A Legacy of Arctic Art

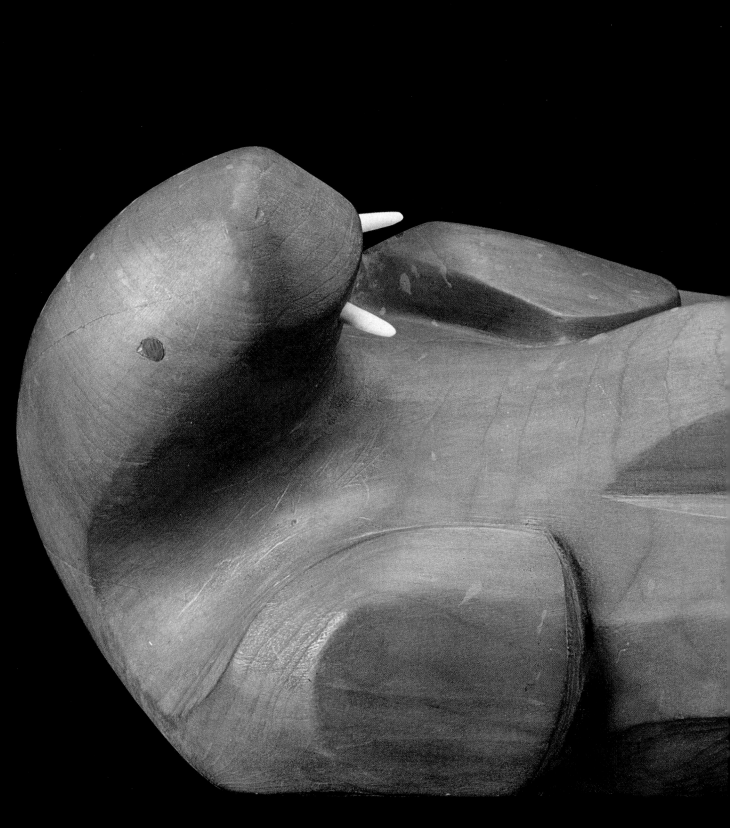

Published for the University of Alaska Museum

A Legacy of Arctic Art

by Dorothy Jean Ray

Foreword by Aldona Jonaitis
Photographs by Barry McWayne

by the University of Washington Press *Seattle and London*

Library of Congress Cataloging in Publication Data
Ray, Dorothy Jean.
    A legacy of arctic art / by Dorothy Jean Ray; foreword by Aldona Jonaitis;
    photographs by Barry McWayne.
      p. cm.
    Includes bibliographical references and index.
    ISBN 0-295-97507-5 (alk. paper)
      1. Eskimo art—Catalogs. 2. Eskimos—Material culture—Catalogs.
    3. University of Alaska Museum—Ethnological collections—Catalogs.
    I. Title.
    E99.E7R34 1996
    704' .03971—dc20   95-36452
                                                                     CIP

The paper used in this publication meets the minimum requirements
of American National Standard for Information Sciences
—Permanence of Paper for Printed Library Materials,
ANSI Z39.48-1984.

Published simultaneously in Canada by Douglas & McIntyre Ltd.

This catalog has been published in conjunction with the exhibition,
A Legacy of Arctic Art, at the University of Alaska Museum, Fairbanks, Alaska,
June–November 1996.
    Major support for this exhibition and publication has been provided
by Holland America Line -Westours, Inc.
    The exhibition has been organized by the University
of Alaska Museum, with support from the City
of Fairbanks Hotel-Motel Tax Fund.

Aldona Jonaitis, Director
Molly Lee, Curator of Ethnology
Barry J. McWayne,
    Coordinator of Fine Arts
Terry P. Dickey,
    Coordinator
    of Education
Wanda W. Chin,
    Coordinator
    of Exhibits

Title pages illustration: Peter J.
Seeganna, King Island. Walrus
sculpture. Wood with baleen
eyes, ivory tusks. 1968. Length
8¼" (see figure 44)

Anonymous, Kuskokwim
River. Spoon. Wood painted
red; mythological figure in
black. Nineteenth century.
17½" (see figure 38)

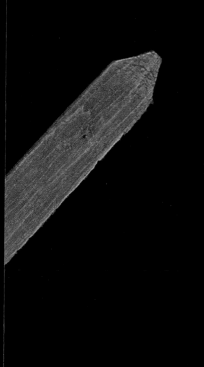

Contents

Foreword

Aldona Jonaitis
Director, University of Alaska Museum

Back in the early 1970s, a group of Columbia University graduate students of what was then infelicitously termed "primitive art" periodically met to discuss bibliographies for the dreaded oral examinations we had to pass before embarking on dissertation research and writing. Those of us who concentrated on Native American art knew we needed two books in order to prepare for questions on Alaskan Eskimo art: Dorothy Jean Ray's *Artists of the Tundra and the Sea* (1961) and *Eskimo Masks: Art and Ceremony* (1967). Nothing else available at that time compared to these detailed, scholarly, and handsomely illustrated studies. When I began teaching Native American art survey courses, I depended for material on Eskimo art upon these wonderful books, as well as upon Ray's subsequent publications: *The Eskimos of Bering Strait, 1650–1898* (1975); *Eskimo Art: Tradition and Innovation in North Alaska* (1977); *Aleut and Eskimo Art: Tradition and Innovation in South Alaska* (1981); and *Ethnohistory in the Arctic: The Bering Strait Eskimo* (1983).

Ray's books reveal to their readers a wealth of impeccably researched information on Eskimo art. Some of this is otherwise available only in older, poorly illustrated monographs, such as John Murdoch's *Ethnological Results of the Point Barrow Expedition* (1892), and Edward Nelson's *The Eskimo About Bering Strait* (1899), both published by the Bureau of American Ethnology. Complementing her well-documented accounts of Eskimo art is a vast body of knowledge acquired from decades of experience with Alaskan Natives and their art.

Robert Mayokok, Wales. Trinket box. Wood with India ink drawings on sides and top. 1968. Height: 3⁵⁄₁₆" (see figure 8)

A Legacy of Arctic Art, a lively memoir of Ray's experiences as a lifelong student of Alaskan Eskimo art, adds a new dimension to her contributions. Some academics equate objectivity with sound scholarship and avoid any forays into subjectivity. This, unfortunately, denies the passions that vitalize their studies, overlooks the delights that accompany any sort of intellectual discovery, and obscures the more personal motivations that lie behind academic investigations. Dorothy Jean Ray is a very different kind of scholar. In this intellectual autobiography, we learn of the inspirations behind her impressive list of books, of her fieldwork in western Alaska, where she met many exceptional Native artists, and of the pleasures that accompanied museum, archive, and library work, which in one place she equates with "playing detective in a mystery that has the right ending." Dorothy Jean Ray, the undisputed authority on Alaskan Eskimo art, writes with genuineness and warmth of the men and women she met, the relationships she formed, and the art they gave or sold to her.

This book also addresses an important issue concerning Native art—the nature of authenticity. According to what I like to call the "purity paradigm," to which many scholars have until recently adhered, the most appropriate subjects of serious research in ethnographic art are those specimens made for "traditional" use. The older the item, the less "sullied" by non-Native influences, the better. Such a perspective denies the value of acculturated art, which it judges to be less authentic, less purely "Native" than its traditional counterparts. Happily, this paradigm has become obsolete, as most scholars today accept that many forms of creative expression offer interesting and useful insights into Native culture.

Once considered completely unworthy of serious academic study, art made by Natives and sold to tourists has become a topic of major interest to contemporary researchers. Our new curator of ethnology here at the University of Alaska Museum, anthropologist Molly Lee, has produced significant scholarship on Alaskan tourist art. My art historical colleague, Ruth Phillips, has not only written extensively on woodlands tourist art, but has also co-edited a book on tourist art around the world with Christopher Steiner, himself an expert on African tourist art. Nelson Graburn's 1976 *Ethnic and Tourist Arts: Cultural Expressions from the Fourth World* has been cited repeatedly as the first major publication on this topic. Although I do not wish to diminish the considerable impact of Graburn's work, it is necessary to point out how well ahead of her time Dorothy Jean Ray was when she published her first book, *Artists of the Tundra and the Sea.*

Bernard Tuglamena Katexac, King Island. *Girl with a Sheefish.* Woodcut in color. 1972. 17" by 7½" (see figure 21)

31/100 GIRL with a SHEEFISH   Bernard Katexac — 72

Fifteen years before Graburn's publications, Ray included, along with the more traditional engraved walrus tusks, items made strictly for sale, such as ivory salt and pepper shakers and billikens. Since that 1961 groundbreaking work, Ray has consistently treated "souvenir" pieces as "authentic" and as interesting as, for example, shaman masks.

Always an independent spirit, Dorothy Jean Ray has not been one to adhere to anyone else's definition of what should and should not be included in a book on Eskimo art. This publication takes us well beyond the conventional in terms of its subject matter. For example, in one case Ray focuses upon an artist whose innovations were not at first fully appreciated. I particularly liked this account of Peter J. Seeganna's wooden walrus, "one of the best sculptures made by an Inupiat man of this century." Ray saw this carving in Nome, on a

Margaret Johnsson, Unalakleet. Eskimo scene. Felt appliqué and embroidery on fabric. 1960s. 16" by 20" (see figure 33)

Viva Wesley, Mekoryuk, Nunivak Island. Doll. Coiled grass basketry with fur accessories. 1978. Height 7½" (see figure 29)

table set up for tourists. Seeganna had carved this unusual piece, which diverged from the standard canons of Eskimo style, and was conducting an "experiment" to see if any tourist would buy it. Happily for Ray, not one of the 600 tourists who visited Nome that week purchased his sculpture, which she then acquired for her own collection.

While scholars may have struggled with questions of the authenticity of objects made by Natives, acculturated or not, they have largely ignored genuinely inauthentic "Eskimo" pieces (as oxymoronic as that may initially sound). Dorothy Jean Ray includes in this book a rather remarkable array of the kinds of fakes that have unfortunately inundated the Native art market: plastic "scrimshaw"; carvings mass-produced in Seattle; even copies of nineteenth-century graphics engraved on 1,000-year-old artifacts by today's scrimshanders. To her surprise, Ray found these objects in a store. Great scholar that she is, she recognized that the images incised on their surfaces had been copied from Hoffman's classic "Graphic Art of the Eskimos." I found these accounts both amusing and disquieting: amusing because of the cockeyed juxtaposition of crass consumerism and refined Eskimo graphics, disquieting because of the unapologetic appropriation of Alaskan Native culture for commercial gains. Ray has done us all a service by bringing these fakes to our attention.

The University of Alaska owes Dorothy Jean Ray a great deal. She has donated to the Rasmuson Library here on the Fairbanks campus her invaluable scholarly archives, and she has enriched our Museum with a remarkable collection of art (along with a small array of well-documented fakes). These pieces, masterfully photographed by Barry McWayne, the Museum's fine arts coordinator, provide clear evidence of the significance of her gift, which has strengthened our already impressive Eskimo art holdings. Her book, *A Legacy of Arctic Art,* serves as a unique catalogue to this collection and contributes in a most moving and informative way to our understanding of Alaskan Eskimo art.

Margaret Johnsson, Unalakleet.
Doll parka. Sealskin with trim
and insets of calfskin. 1966.
Length 18½" (see figure 32)

Preface

This book describes the Native art and artifacts in the collection that I donated to the University of Alaska Museum. It is essentially a catalog for an exhibition, but it departs somewhat from the usual catalog in being also a history of my dual role as a collector and an anthropologist. My descriptions of each piece combine formal analysis with a more or less informal discussion of the personal relationships with the artists or donors from whom I obtained the objects over a period of almost fifty years.

I acquired this collection in the course of my research of Native Alaskan cultures, especially Eskimo art and ethnohistory. Every piece has a special meaning to me, and because these objects have been so much integrated with my research and writing, I could not imagine their going separate ways to an auction house or dealer's shop. Rather I envisioned them as a family—in one place, preferably in a museum where a wider audience could share them. I chose the University of Alaska Museum in Fairbanks as the most appropriate home for this collection, not only because the university has a vital Native arts and culture program but because my papers, notes, and photographs pertaining to this collection and my related research are destined for the university archives.

Anonymous, St. Michael Bucket, said to have been owned by Chief Tugalina. Wood. Late nineteenth century. Height 9½" (see figure 39)

A brief account of my research and writings and the changes that have taken place in Eskimo culture, especially the arts, sets the stage for discussion of each object in the catalog. Although I have illustrated some of the objects in the collection in my previous publications, they are presented here from a different perspective. There is,

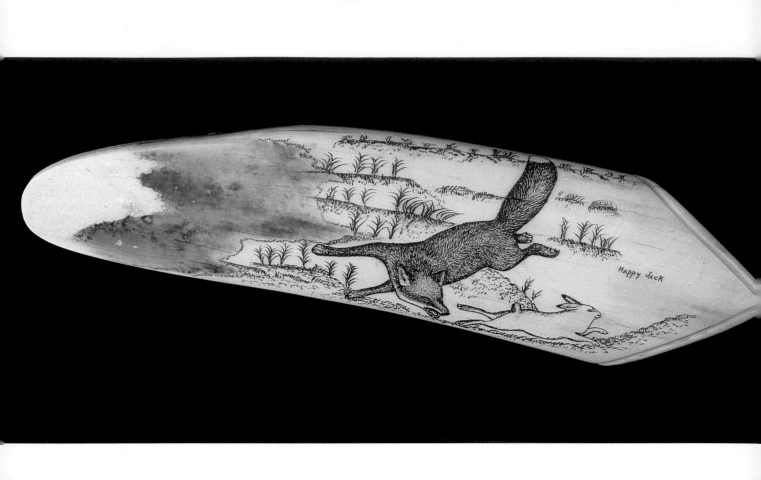

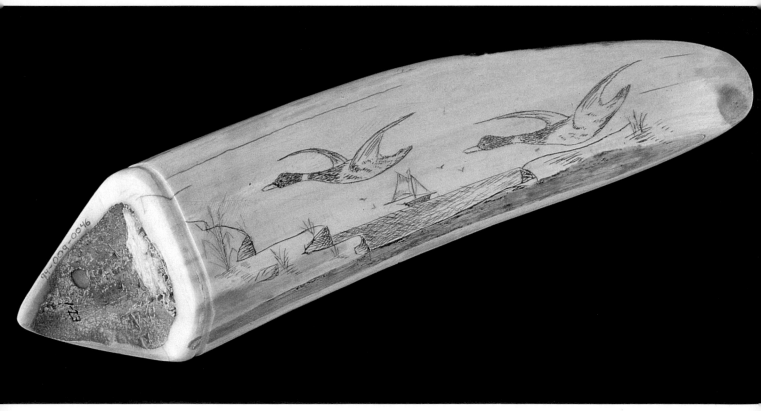

furthermore, a great deal of new material, including three unusually excellent examples of noted carver Happy Jack's work, never before published; an account of the Federal Trade Commission hearing on spurious Native objects (1975); a discussion (and illustrations) of copies and fakes of Eskimo objects; and a rare collection of the earliest Canadian Inuit soapstone carvings (1952). Several contemporary artists are here, including George Ahgupuk (his rare Deers Press book of drawings and commentary of 1953); Bernard Katexac (his thoughts on the making of two of his prints in this collection); and Robert Mayokok (further data about an Eskimo man successful in an alien culture). Also, Shafter Toshavik and Margaret Johnsson gave me new information about the Inviting-In Feast of 1912.

The principal part of the collection consists of engraved ivory that dates from 1866 (a documented piece from the Western Union Telegraph Expedition) to the present, with half a dozen Happy Jack pieces, which to my knowledge is the largest Happy Jack collection in any museum. But it also includes artifacts that have a significance for me beyond mere acquisition: some I received as gifts; others I purchased for their unusual place in history, or for unique circumstances, or as a token of friendship with an artist. These items include (among others): a berry bucket that was said to have been owned by Tugalina, the last chief of St. Michael; a birch bark snuff box that was given to me by Emma Willoya, an Eskimo woman who had devoted her life to helping her fellow Eskimos; a driftwood walrus made by King Island artist Peter J. Seeganna for a remarkable experiment in 1968; a doll parka of exquisite design made by Margaret Johnsson, a Yup'ik woman, and an original notebook of picture writing to remember the Scriptures, invented by Ruth Ekak, the mother of Lily Savok, who gave me the booklet.

You will discover, as you browse through the catalog, that the brief caption with each figured object includes the name of the artist, when known, followed by the object, its medium, and its dimension in inches, height preceding width. The narrative text offers more extensive description of each piece, along with all available background details, and is keyed to the figure number of the object. Throughout the book, formal description is integrated with interpretive commentary as well as discussions of personal associations with the artist—to the extent known. With respect to these personal aspects, knowledge is limited to recent and present times, of course. Because such insights are so significant for evaluation and appreciation of Native art, I have placed the section treating contemporary graphic art first. I have chosen this arrangement

Happy Jack, Nome. Walrus ivory mattock head. A and B: reverse sides shown. Engraved with a fox and a rabbit on one side; flying geese on the other. Before 1918. 9¾" (see figure 54)

because we know the motivations, attitudes, and life histories for many of these artists, whereas such information is totally lacking for those living in archeological and long-ago times, and we are thus deprived of direct critical insights. Nonetheless, we can infer from our knowledge of recent lives much that illuminates the intrinsic aspects of Eskimo art without respect to time.

No reference to "theory" will be made here, because that term, in its ordinary usage, is inappropriate in this context. Tentative interpretations, yes; theory, no. A few years ago I was surprised by a colleague's statement that she had finally begun to take an interest in objects, having previously been interested only in theory. At the time it seemed that she was criticizing projects pertaining to material culture, but later, I decided that perhaps she realized that the study of artifacts went beyond description of objects to involve a people's history, culture, survival, recreation, ceremony, and sometimes religion; in short, everything that makes a life. Yet, an object is sometimes just there as a thing of beauty, or as something that reaches out for a response, something that speaks to you from the man or woman who made it. Almost all collectors of Native American art whom I know have begun their collections in this way—out of love for the art—but I also know a few who collect as investment for future profit. Such stockpiling is especially tempting today, with sales of indigenous arts commanding ever higher figures. This is a two-edged sword, for while the seller makes a handsome profit, selling prices are sometimes so high that museums on a limited budget cannot buy even one object that would fill a gap in their holdings.

Perhaps this is just as well, one may say, because it has been argued that the fewer objects a museum has, the better, especially if it lacks facilities to place them on public view. I've heard many a complaint about certain objects buried in museum storage, yet those very objects often do make their way to the public via research and publication by anthropologists and art historians. If a museum is secure and safe from fire, I think that it cannot have too many objects. They preserve the past and provide for the pleasure and education of generations to come.

What do we call these things that we put in a museum—art, artifacts, objects, crafts, souvenirs? I have always used the term "art" in its broadest sense; that is, as a product resulting from creativity, ingenuity, and good craftsmanship. Today there seems to be a need to separate the "fine art" made by the young men and women who have studied formal art in workshops and universities from what has been called "souvenir art," made mostly by self-taught artists.

There is no problem with that division, although the two can over-lap. One could scarcely mistake one of Aleut artist John Hoover's elegant ten-foot-tall sculptures for a souvenir, yet an equally "fine arts" sculpture, a wooden walrus by Peter Seeganna (fig. 44) overlaps into the blurred boundary of the souvenir, as we shall see later.

The term "fine arts" has a solid base; the difficulty is in what to call all of those objects made to sell as—well, let's call them—souvenirs. Several names have been proposed to categorize these objects. The term "souvenir art" has sometimes been regarded as an oxymoron, but I do not think that there is a much better term, espe-cially if we can rid ourselves of the idea that "souvenir equals gim-mick," and replace it with "souvenir equals memento." This, after all, is what art is about. I coined the term "market art," which has been used occasionally, most notably by J. G. E. Smith in his *Arctic Art: Eskimo Ivory,* but I still think that the term "souvenir art" is equally good. Other terms such as "tourist art" and "airport art" have been proposed by Nelson H. H. Graburn, but both of these terms have a limited scope and deny a long tradition of the art and its historic audience, in Alaska, at least. The people who bought sou-venir objects early on were rarely tourists, and Alaska then had no airports. They were usually people working in Alaska, who, upon leaving, desired mementos of a unique country. Today, in the 1990s, Eskimo art has changed greatly from the earliest works, and, in addi-tion, many collectors now recognize both the beauty of the contem-porary fine art and the historic significance and artistic merit of a number of the objects sold as souvenirs.

I am using the name "Eskimo" interchangeably with "Inupiaq" (plural, Inupiat) and "Yup'ik" (plural, Yupiit), which are favored today because these words mean "the people" in their own language. The word "Eskimo" supposedly originated from an Algon-quian Indian term meaning "eater of raw meat," and has been con-sidered—wrongly, I think—to be a pejorative term. The name has a long and honorable history and should not be discarded.

In Canada, the term "Inuit" is appropriate because all speak the same language. In Alaska, however, the Inupiat (northern Eskimos) speak a language that, at its geographical extremes, is unintelligible to the Yupiit (southern Eskimos). Therefore, when we speak of Alaskan Eskimos as a whole, it is more economical to say "Eskimo." My old Eskimo friends in Nome settled this terminology to their own satisfaction: they weren't Eskimo or Inupiaq; they were "Native," and proud of it!

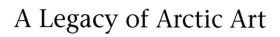

A Legacy of Arctic Art

How It Started and Where It Went

I saw Nome for the first time in darkness, with the wind whipping up a blizzard when the Pan Am DC–3 landed with a nifty glide one December night in 1945. My memory of that night is vague because I was still queasy from the trip on the old SS *Yukon* from Seattle to Seward, but I know that I awoke the next morning in a foreign country. What I didn't know was that this was the place that would put me on the track of research and writing for the rest of my life. I walked around that woebegone town on the edge of a frozen sea, with houses and shacks built every which way right up to the street, some tilted into the permafrost with no paint and no yard, quite unlike the lushness and tidiness of places I had called home in Iowa, Florida, and California. I have been told that people either love Nome or hate it—there is no in-between—and after a few weeks, despite the raw wind stinging with snow, the endless expanse of tundra, the darkness closing down early in the afternoon like a heavy quilt, I knew that this was a place where I could live—and like it—because I had discovered another dimension, the very heart of Nome: its people.

The population at that time was about equally divided between Caucasians and people of Eskimo heritage, but race relations were not always on an even keel. After the discovery of gold in 1898, Nome began as a white man's settlement near an Eskimo fishing site. The nearest permanent village, Ayasayuk, was at Cape Nome, twelve miles to the east. When the tens of thousands of prospectors and other would-be

3

millionaires came to Nome during the gold rush of 1900, Eskimos from nearby islands and coastal villages also came to trade, sometimes to work, and always to sell their handicrafts. Many returned to their homes at the end of summer, but some families became permanent residents. From early days Eskimos had intermarried with the newcomers; yet a subtle and sometimes flagrant discrimination persisted. Before a remarkable law, popularly called the "Equal Rights Bill," was passed by the Territorial Legislature in February 1945, only a few months before I arrived in Nome, the Eskimos could not eat in the restaurants, stay in the hotels, or sit wherever they wished in the cinema. That changed with the law, but change does not come overnight. As late as 1950 they still tended to sit in their old places in the Dream Theater. On the surface, life in Nome seemed to be calm enough in 1945, but beneath it ran all of the past hurts, the various ethnic factions (a strange threesome of Caucasian, full-blood Eskimos, and part-blood Eskimos), and the growing boldness of activism among the younger Eskimos.

I soon found, however, a constant in this town—the dazzling displays of ivory carvings in so many of the stores. Looking back almost fifty years to my first acquaintance with this art, so different from what I had known before, I often think about the Eskimo carvers who were creating such marvels at that time but who had no place in Nome society; and about some of the Nome residents who considered these carvings as nothing but curios. Also, as I look back it is tempting to say that I set out on the study path of Eskimo art and history from the moment I set eyes on the ivory; but the truth is, I didn't have the slightest inkling that it would eventually take me to so many libraries, archives, and museums, and thence to the people themselves. I was more interested in skiing, fishing for tomcods and king crabs, and looking for a job. (One of my jobs, at the post office, gave me a crash course in place names and personal names of northwest Alaska.) But right from the start, I did try to find information about the carvers and their work (as well as about other contemporary Native art) in Nome's tiny library and in private libraries, without success. However, I found a few books on archeology, and a beat-up copy of E. W. Nelson's *The Eskimo About Bering Strait* was given to me by Otto W. Geist, the collector of archeological and paleontological materials at the University of Alaska, who was temporarily in Nome waiting for transportation to Fairbanks at the end of his wartime career with the Alaska Territorial Guard. A large part of the ten-thousand artifacts collected by Nelson between 1877 and 1881 (now in the Smithsonian Institution) was illustrated in that book, which Otto called his "bible," and by the time I left Nome in 1947 I had memorized almost every object in the book. But these were artifacts collected almost seventy years before, not contemporary objects.

When I returned to Nome for a few months in 1950, for a study of Native/non-Native relations (but not for a study of ivory carving!), with a small grant from the Arctic Institute of North America, after more than a year's study at Harvard, I was approached by Antonio (Tony) Polet with a proposition he thought I couldn't turn down: that I buy his retail shop (Polet's Arts and Crafts), which he had built on Front Street after selling his huge store on the west end. Polet, who was born in Italy, was one of the real old-timers. He had arrived in Nome in 1900 at the age of nineteen with a stock of groceries. In the 1940s his big store was stocked not only with basic merchandise and food needed in the North but also with large quantities of ivory and fur products. The carvers and seamstresses worked right on the premises. Polet knew of my interest in the Eskimo handicrafts; after all, I had haunted his old store, and perhaps he thought that my surviving a whole year as proprietor of a tiny restaurant a few years before had qualified me as an ivory merchant. But admiring these handicrafts and selling them were in two different worlds to me at that time. I not only wanted to continue my graduate studies, but I had a dim view of the buying tactics of some of my would-be business rivals, who, according to some of my Eskimo friends, had treated them quite shabbily.

I moved to Fairbanks that same year, and at the University of Alaska my rather amorphous idea about ivory carving research took on a sharper focus. Although I was not involved directly with the anthropology department (I was employed at the Geophysical Institute), I joined in the enthusiasm that the people in the department had for the new discipline of arctic studies. Although a few pioneers such as Margaret Lantis, Frederica de Laguna, Henry Collins, J. L. (Louis) Giddings, Cornelius Osgood, W. S. Laughlin, and Froelich Rainey were already well known for their researches in the North, few universities had courses devoted to the Arctic. At Harvard I had taken the only "northern" course offered that year—on the peoples of Siberia—but the University of Alaska, despite its small enrollment then, had three courses: a year-long course in arctic archeology; "Peoples of the Arctic" (first semester); and "Alaskan Natives" (second semester). Although the latter course was designed "primarily for students who expected to teach in native schools," the existence of such a course implied that there was a laboratory out there in the vastness of Alaska—"native schools,"indeed—with unlimited possibilities.

The early 1950s at the University of Alaska was a heady time of plans and projects aimed at bringing the unknown of the vast Alaska laboratory into the known. The teachers, guest lecturers, and students at that time made invaluable contributions to northern archeology and ethnology: Louis Giddings, William Irving, Charles Lucier, Margaret Lantis, Helge Larsen, Wendell Oswalt, and James W. VanStone. (I suppose that I can include myself as a student, since I enrolled in the year-long arctic archeology course when it was taught by VanStone.) Otto Geist had an office and laboratory on campus. He and Ivar Skarland, the head of the anthropology department and the only anthropology teacher until VanStone arrived, kept interest simmering with their ideas and their knowledge of the country. Otto had collected valuable ethnological information during his archeological visits to St. Lawrence Island in the 1920s and 1930s, and Lorraine Donoghue Koranda in the music department began recording Eskimo songs and dances (Koranda 1972).

Armed with the optimism of pioneers and with the confidence that there would be enough "arctic anthropologists" to supply papers on an "irregular" basis, Skarland, VanStone, and Oswalt founded the journal, *Anthropological Papers of the University of Alaska.* The first issue was published in December 1952, with papers by J. L. Giddings, Jr., Robert F. Heizer, W. S. Laughlin, and Wendell Oswalt. The first issues (usually two a year) were in a small size, six by nine inches, but beginning in 1974 the format was enlarged to eight and a half by eleven.

By the time I had decided to return to graduate school—this time at the University of Washington—I still had found only one article on the subject of contemporary northern Eskimo art: a discussion of ivory bracelets by Albert C. Heinrich, who had taught on Little Diomede Island (Heinrich 1950). There was, however, a book on Yup'ik art by Hans Himmelheber, *Eskimokünstler,* which summarized his research from June 1936 to April 1937 on Nunivak Island and the Kuskokwim River. This was his third fieldwork with non-Western peoples, and after his first publication of *Negerkünstler* in 1935, he was recognized as an expert in African art, a field that he specialized in as ethnologist and art collector after his trip to Alaska. *Eskimokünstler,* first published in 1938 in German and translated into English as *Eskimo Artists* in 1987, is an anecdotal description of his fieldwork—essentially notes from his field workbook—with little summary or critical interpretation. His principal thesis, stated in his very first sentence, that the arts "of the Kuskokwim Eskimo are practiced for the sake of representation, not for aesthetic effect," seems at odds with the beautiful creations that the Yup'ik artists were making, and continue to make (Himmelheber 1993:11).

Himmelheber also expected to extend his research farther north, but after a trip to St. Michael, Nome, and Barrow, he dismissed the Inupiaq ivory carvers merely as curio makers, whose customers' "taste could really be satisfied by any clumsy child's hand" (ibid.:52). He wrote in his preface to the 1953 German edition that a study of art was no longer possible in northern Alaska, and comments throughout his monograph categorize the Yup'ik artisans as "artists," but the Inupiaq as "curio makers" (1953:7).[1] He had, however, ignored the fact that, long before he visited the Kuskokwim Eskimos, they had also copied western forms and sold souvenirs or "curios." Moravian missionaries were among the collectors after they had established their first mission at Bethel in 1885. Adolph Stecker, who served in Alaska from 1900 to 1927, deposited a number of souvenirs in the Herrnhut Museum, Herrnhut, Germany. Some of the objects, which are illustrated in two papers by the ethnologist Heinz Israel of Dresden, Germany, date from before the turn of the century. The objects range from ivory pipes and cribbage boards with geometric engravings to the kinds of souvenirs that Himmelheber decried in the North: "toothpicks" in the shape of fish, napkin rings, toothpick holders, buttons, crochet hooks, gavels, and spoons and forks, all made of walrus ivory. Cribbage boards were also collected from Nunivak Island as early as the 1910s and are prototypes of the tusks and cribbage boards with the complex intertwined animals, usually referred to as the "Nunivak tusk" (Israel 1961, 1971). These were in full production by Himmelheber's time, because the Lomen Corporation, which had established a reindeer herd on the island, began importing walrus tusks for the carving in the 1920s.

I am discussing the artist–curio maker dichotomy at length because, with the availability of Himmelheber's monograph in English, his viewpoint toward the two appears to be either black or white with no middle ground, but it is obvious that the Yup'ik and Inupiaq artists were both. The northern and southern areas had experienced different rates of acculturation, and Himmelheber was fortunate to be in southwest Alaska while many families were still living a more-or-less traditional lifestyle, but had he expanded his research to the north, he would have found a lifestyle on King Island and Little Diomede Island as "primitive"—maybe more so—

as that in Bethel, where he conducted a large part of his research. By 1955, when I went back to Nome, the lives of the northern carvers, many of whom were from the islands, had changed rapidly.

In 1953 at the University of Washington, I felt both prepared and unprepared to talk to the ivory carvers. Although I was acquainted with objects in illustrations, I had inspected comparatively few at first hand. So I decided to spend a summer in museums. My plan, which I carried out, was to examine Eskimo artifacts in those museums with the largest collections, and to keep a visual record with my new 4x5 Linhof camera. Putting this hobby to work proved to be one of the best decisions I ever made. With my fieldwork on hold, I spent the summer of 1954 examining the collections of the Field Museum in Chicago; the United States National Museum (Smithsonian Institution) in Washington, D.C.; the American Museum of Natural History in New York; the Peabody Museum in Cambridge, Massachusetts; and the University Museum at the University of Pennsylvania in Philadelphia.[2]

The University of Washington gave me a princely grant of $400 to cover all of my expenses, including transportation. By eating soup and indulging in the hospitality of friends, I made it through the summer. It sounds like a fairy tale when I write that a hotel room in New York cost me only five dollars a night, but that is what I paid at the Henry Hudson Hotel. Each evening I had a huge bowl of soup with crusty bread at a wonderful delicatessen nearby. In Philadelphia I stayed with my brother, Ted Tostlebe, and in Washington, D.C., Margaret Lantis unselfishly provided me with both hospitality and encouragement in her Alexandria apartment. It isn't everyone who would give up a bathroom each evening so that I could develop the day's negatives and hang them up to dry! The first evening, Margaret and her mother, who lived nearby, were puzzled as to how I would identify the objects on each negative—one negative had twenty-seven pieces. Luckily, I had brought all my notes home with me so that I could explain the measurements and descriptions I had made for each object and the diagrams for each layout. In retrospect, getting all of that down was the hardest work of my life—in each museum: checking the card catalog; looking at every object in the Eskimo collection; studying each object and evaluating it for my research topic; choosing which to photograph; arranging, measuring, and describing each; arranging the lights; computing the exposure (no built-in light meter then!); and tripping the shutter. I did not attempt any "art" shots—time was precious and I worked full speed. Besides, these were merely photos for my research, and I didn't suspect that I would use so many of them in my books on Eskimo art. I also would have liked to take 35mm color slides, but this would have required different lights and setups, which was impossible in my limited time, even though two of the museums permitted me to work after closing time and on the weekends.

That summer I also had an opportunity to talk to Louis Giddings, another of the established anthropologists who were always willing to give a helping hand to those just starting out. In our discussions of anthropology in general, and my current work specifically, he asked if my study of museum collections was to end as "just a catalog," that is, as description and photographs. He apparently thought this was a deadend kind of study (which, if it had ended there, certainly would have been), but I explained that it was background information for a proposed field study with the ivory carvers, and that I had to acquire as much "hands-on" information about the materials, style, and form of Eskimo art as possible.

I was a teaching assistant at the University of Washington in the fall of 1954, and I shared a telephone via a pass-through with Verne F. Ray, my graduate adviser, in an adjacent office. One day he invited me to lunch, and another, to dinner, and before long Viola Garfield, one of Verne's colleagues, and her husband, Charles Garfield, who had been in Nome during the 1900 gold rush, witnessed our marriage ceremony. My fieldwork, nevertheless, went ahead as planned in 1955. Verne went along, a decision that surely led to second thoughts, because I doubt if he had ever spent a more uncomfortable summer, enduring boredom, rain, mosquitoes, and a broken-down water system. I had received a bigger grant that summer—all of $500!—but again, a friend came to the rescue. Carrie McLain, Nome's resident historian, let us stay rent-free in an old cabin if we paid for the oil and hooked up the water pipes.

In 1955, running water was available only in the summertime, when it was piped in above ground from Moonlight Springs. In the winter, water was delivered in trucks and pumped into a tank or carried into a building by the bucketful. (Nowadays, running water is brought to Nome year-round in heated casements.) For our cabin's water "system," pipe had to be laid a distance of about fifty feet from the main source in the street above the cabin, which was situated at the back end of the beach near what was then the Caterpillar Company. One look at that pile of pipe was enough to send anyone running back to the airport. Many of the pieces were not only cracked but of different sizes! Cutting and threading the pipe turned out to be a test of ingenuity as well as a form of torment, since Verne worked under a constant cloud of mosquitoes that, as I tried to brush them away, merely rearranged themselves over his face and hands.

With the water pipes put together, we turned our attention to the interior of the cabin. We were fortunate to have a place to stay (it was not always easy to find a house or apartment to rent in Nome during the summer), but it did take a lot of time to make the place habitable—fixing and refixing the stove and rearranging the five or six thin mattresses on the bed so that we would not roll off. When the mosquitoes weren't biting, it was raining; and when it wasn't raining, it was blowing; and I suppose the only satisfaction that Verne had that summer was staying dry and warm in the cabin with his own work while I trudged every day in wind and rain to various parts of Nome and to King Island Village, a mile away. The majority of ivory artists in Nome during 1955 were the King Islanders and Little Diomede Islanders, who came to Nome every summer. The community house, a long Quonset hut, which I visited in the village, belonged to the King Islanders, but people from other villages or from Nome came to visit. The building had only two doors, front and back, and one small window at the back, where the men sat on the floor to carve. Usually four or five men, and sometimes a young boy, worked at one time in the building, carving the objects that they placed for sale on a table just inside the front door, which faced the sea. Occasionally, a Coleman lantern dispelled some of the gloom, but even so, it was so dim that even my 35mm Tri-X film could not capture everything. I did not use flash because I wanted to photograph the men working as naturally as possible, although they told me I could use flash bulbs if I wished. (See photographs in Ray 1961, reprinted in 1980.) Aloysius Pikonganna, who spoke English, and the other carvers made me feel welcome in every way.

During the day, customers occasionally came to the building to watch the men work or to buy something, but in the evening, the building bustled with tour groups who came to watch the King Islanders dance and sing, and later, to buy carvings and fur slippers, purses, dolls, and other fur products that were displayed on the front table. Those days are gone. In 1973 a storm wiped out almost all of King Island Village, the community house with it, and the King Islanders dispersed permanently to other towns, especially Nome, after their school on the island was condemned. All of the carvers of that summer are dead—I had a happy reunion with Aloysius in Nome in 1986 a few months before his death—but their works still live. My book, *Artists of the Tundra and the Sea,* gives an account of that summer.

Although my original interest in Eskimo culture was the art, I was also interested in history, geography, and tribal land use. This focus intensified through discussions with Verne, who, in the 1930s, had written a number of papers and monographs on political organization and land use of western Indian tribes, and was serving as a consultant and expert witness for various tribes before the U.S. Court of Claims and the Indian Claims Commission. As I tried to find publications on subsistence and land use for the Bering Strait area, I was faced with the same problem as when I had searched for information on contemporary Eskimo art—there wasn't anything. Mainly to satisfy my own curiosity, I began mapping old villages and tribal boundaries and recording historical data from old-timers in 1961. It grew into a full-fledged project during my field trip of 1964, the results of which I combined with explorers' observations to write the first summaries and interpretations of land use and tribal boundaries in the Bering Strait area: "Nineteenth Century Settlement and Subsistence Patterns in Bering Strait" (1964), and "Land Tenure and Polity of the Bering Strait Eskimos" (1967a).[3]

These two papers had given me an idea for another manuscript, again to fill a gap in my own knowledge: this was to be an historical overview of the Bering Strait area from the dual perspective of the Eskimos and the foreign forces that had accumulated to produce changes in Eskimo culture. The general histories of Alaska were mostly chronological accounts of ships and places. They rarely mentioned what the explorers or early travelers had learned about the inhabitants. It was almost as if the Eskimos did not exist in Alaska's histories. Since many of the earliest reports were in Russian, I managed to teach myself enough of the language to know when I needed help. One of my helpers when I lived in Washington, D.C., was Rhea Josephson, a Russian-born, American-trained lawyer, who came to my rescue many times when I was reading the Russian accounts so essential to my research at the Library of Congress and National Archives. I carried out further fieldwork for this proposed book, an ethnohistory, in 1968 in St. Michael, Unalakleet, Nome, and Wales (Alaska!), and in several other localities, but my stay in Unalakleet remains most vivid in my memory. I have only the fondest memories and admiration for the people who so willingly helped me—in fact, cooperated with me—in writing their history.

All of the people of Unalakleet were welcoming and friendly, and they did not seem perturbed that I was only one of several other anthropologists there that summer. I worked with the older people because of the nature of the information that I needed, and I had to disappoint several younger men who eagerly lined up. I stayed with Marion Gonangnan (known as Mrs. Myles, after her late husband's first name), who provided me with all of the comforts of civilization—a bed with an innerspring mattress, a down comforter, two big pillows, a table and chairs, and a desk. In her spacious kitchen she displayed some of her favorite possessions: row upon row of teapots and sweet-smelling soap! Of all the people in Unalakleet, I was closest to Marion's daughter, Martha (Mrs. Peter) Nanouk, who was always willing to answer any question and who also invited me many times to eat the delicacies of the Arctic—blueberries, reindeer stew, or dried fish. Marion's and Martha's family had an illustrious ancestor, Alluyianuk (Martha's great-grandfather), a Malemiut man who was known as a chief and who had helped members of the Western Union Telegraph Expedition in the mid 1860s. The engraved wand or snow beater in figure 45 dates from the time of that expedition.

I also became well acquainted with Thora Katchatag, who sold me Chief Tugalina's berry bucket (fig. 39). I had visited Thora at her fishing camp, *Chauiyak* (Eskimo drum), in 1964 and again in 1968. One of the high points of that summer was going with her and her son to their favorite salmonberry patch, where, after we had filled our buckets and were turning for home, she knelt down and gave thanks to the universe and to God for providing such bounty. Thora's son also took me in his boat to Egavik, where I visited Hazel Kotongan (Thora's sister) and her husband John, and to the cozy, parklike summer camp of Jacob Kenick, whom I mention in the Scripture writing (figs. 25 and 26).[4]

Although acquiring new information is a most satisfying part of field research, it was also rewarding to meet people about whom I had read in historical sources. One of these persons was Shafter Toshavik of Unalakleet (born in St. Michael), who had been one of the unidentified messengers in E. W. Hawkes's *The 'Inviting-In' Feast of the Alaskan Eskimo,* a report of the Unalakleet–St. Michael Messenger Feast of 1912 (Hawkes 1913). Shafter, who said he had acquired his first name from a bag of potatoes, had grown up as an orphan, living from family to family, to become a considerate, dignified man. Although Hawkes did not name any participants in the ceremony of 1912, I have identified several of them from information given to me by both Toshavik and Margaret Johnsson, who also attended the festivities, in my discussion of the wooden mask shown in figure 42. (See also fig. 32, Margaret Johnsson's doll parka.)

The summer of 1968 I met several other men who were mentioned in early accounts and who brought history right to my doorstep. Two of the men, Simon Sagoonik of Nome and George Ootenna of Wales, had been young reindeer herders in the 1890s, and Arthur Nagozruk, Sr., also from Wales, had been mentioned in Bureau of Education reports for 1904 and 1905 as a bright lad from whom great things were expected. Indeed, he had retired in Nome after a successful career as one of Alaska's first Eskimo teachers.

My voluminous field and archival notes were finally distilled into a manageable book of more than 300 pages, *The Eskimos of Bering Strait, 1650–1898*. Of necessity, the book omitted many details that I had included in earlier papers. Therefore, Richard A. Pierce, whose Limestone Press has enriched our knowledge of Alaska history, especially during the Russian period, proposed that I collect my papers for publication in his series. Published as *Ethnohistory in the Arctic: The Bering Strait Eskimo* (1983), it complements *The Eskimos of Bering Strait* and also includes several papers that extend beyond 1898.[5]

Just as I was beginning my ethnohistorical research, I received a letter from Alfred A. Blaker, who was then head of the Scientific Photographic Laboratory at the University of California in Berkeley. Blaker asked if I would write a text to go with photographs he had taken of masks in the Lowie Museum collection. The masks had captured his interest when he took his undergraduate degree in anthropology.[6] He had inquired first of Edward Keithahn, director of the Alaska State Museum in Juneau, who steered him to me because I had earlier studied the many masks in the Juneau museum. When I began my Eskimo art research, mask making was almost a thing of the past, which is difficult to believe now, since it has become one of the favorite revivals of a new generation of artists who are making masks by the dozens. But in 1955, the King Islanders carved only two masks—both by Tony Pushruk—which we bought.

Al Blaker's request was a challenge I could not resist: to write the first summary account of Alaskan Eskimo masks and their ceremonial context to accompany his excellent photographs, taken in both color and black-and-white. With his permission, I added a few photographs of my own and reprinted the plates of masks in Nelson's *The Eskimo About Bering Strait* to illustrate as many kinds of masks as possible. This book, *Eskimo Masks: Art and Ceremony,* which was published in 1967 and reprinted as a paperback in 1975, and in a Danish edition in 1970, has been out-of-print for some time. Of all my books, it is the one most often asked (begged!) for (Ray and Blaker 1967). Alfred Blaker left the University of California for a career of teaching and writing on photography, and my sister-in-law Marilyn Hanson, who has a degree in art, has told me that there is no better book on the fundamentals of photography than his *Photography: Art and Technique* (1980).

I had plans to write a second volume of the ethnohistory, dating from 1898 when gold was discovered near Nome, but it was postponed (forever, it seems) by an idea that had been simmering for some time: writing an illustrated history of Alaskan Eskimo art during the historical and contemporary periods. Even by the 1970s there was little information about Eskimo art, aside from my books and articles and a few exhibition catalogs and general books on Indians such as *Indian Art in America* (Dockstader 1960), which usually illustrated a few token masks and ivory carvings, the same ones sometimes to be repeated in similar books.[7] My photography hobby came in handy again, for, although I had examples of historical objects from my 1954 museum foray, I had only a few photos of contemporary works. By then, however, I had a small artifact collection of my own, but more important, I had friends whose Alaskan collections, put together, represented the entire range of men's and women's handicrafts. With only a few exceptions, I photographed the collections in their homes, where they also gave me bed and breakfast, all of which went beyond simple friendship, and for which I shall be grateful forever. After I had organized the photographs and notes for my text, I realized that the material was too extensive for one volume, so I divided it into two: one for the northern or Inupiaq people north of St. Michael (*Eskimo Art: Tradition and Innovation in North Alaska*); and the other, for the southern peoples, including the Yup'ik, Aleut, Alutiq, and the Cordova area (*Aleut and Eskimo Art: Tradition and Innovation in South Alaska*).

While I was working on the Eskimo art history, I was also involved in another project as editorial co-author with Louis L. Renner, S. J., for a biography of the pioneer missionary Bellarmine Lafortune (Renner 1979). I had jumped at the chance to work with Fr. Renner, not only because he was writing history at its purest—almost exclusively from archival sources—but because the subject of Alaskan missions needed to be explored, and he was the foremost authority on Catholic history in Alaska. The establishing of the many different denominational missions was closely related to western education of Eskimos in the late nineteenth and early twentieth centuries, and to the rates of cultural change that missionaries and teachers brought to the villages. I had written a chapter about missions and schools in *The Eskimos of Bering Strait,* and here was my chance to increase my knowledge of the Catholic effort, especially if I were to write "Volume 2" of the ethnohistory, because Catholic missions began at Bering Strait only after the gold rush.

Working on this manuscript rekindled my interest in the post–gold rush missions in the Nome area, and—I suppose still with hopes of writing that albatross "Volume 2"—I dug up my National Archives notes about a Methodist mission that had been established in 1906 at Sinuk, a village northwest of Nome, in an effort to lure the Eskimos away from Nome, more especially, away from the liquor trade. I had not known of the existence of the mission until I discovered the manuscript materials in the Archives, and it had never been mentioned in any general publications. Its success was variable over the years, as both children and adults were taught basic routines of western civilization as well as some religion. It was a haven for twenty-two orphans after the influenza epidemic of 1918, but it was abandoned in 1919 after a fire destroyed the building and two of the children died (Ray 1984c).

When I began my study of the Eskimo arts in the 1950s, I did not dream that I would receive so many requests for information from people who had read my books and articles. Queries about Happy Jack, the famous gold-rush carver, and about the billiken, a good-luck piece adopted by the ivory carvers in 1909, topped the list, yet both subjects were but a minute portion of my writing. In the early 1970s, the editors of the *Alaska Journal* thought it about time that I bring the billiken story up to date (I had written about the billiken for the *Alaska Sportsman* in 1960). The billiken, whose adventures I summarize later in this book (figs. 76–79), was still a popular souvenir item in 1974, when my article was published, but now, twenty years later, its popularity has diminished. Nonetheless, I still receive letters from people wanting more information, especially so they can write a book about it. I have found it fascinating to reconstruct its history, especially its economic importance to the ivory carvers, but its artistic merit is about zero, so I am hopeful that writing about the billiken has run its course.

Happy Jack's engraving on ivory is in a different dimension. The glowing reports that had preceded my first look at his pieces were certainly justified. I wrote about him for the first time in *Artists of the Tundra and the Sea* (1961), which precipitated a flood of inquiries from people who thought they had a "Happy Jack." By the early 1980s I decided to write a more comprehensive article about Happy

Jack for *American Indian Art Magazine,* so that the growing number of Happy Jack collectors could do a little homework on their own. The article, "Happy Jack: King of the Eskimo Ivory Carvers" (1984a), generated more interest than ever. Although people continued to write to me for information, I also acquired more examples of Happy Jack's works, enough to warrant an updated article about this remarkable artist: "Happy Jack and his Artistry" (1989). After publication of the second article, I purchased three unusual tusks, which are included in this collection (figs. 53–58) and are here published for the first time. Further information about Happy Jack and his work can be found on pages 115–30.

I have been asked which of my projects is my favorite. It is like asking which of your children you like best. I can say truthfully that all of them qualify as "favorite"; yet there are several peaks among the favorites—projects that I now realize involved a considerable amount of detective work, or addressed misconceptions, or "set the record straight." I played the sleuth to discover the meaning of the symbols in "picture writing," which was used by Eskimos to remember hymns and the Scriptures. Lily Savok, who gave me her mother's notebook (fig. 25), and I spent many hours reconstructing the history of the picture writing and recording why certain symbols were used to remind a person of the Eskimo translation.

Another favorite is the so-called Kheuveren Legend. In this legend, some Russian writers (and even Americans) believed that a Russian settlement had existed in the Bering Strait area before Alaska was discovered by Vitus Bering in 1741. This village was supposedly established by sailors in a boat unaccounted for during Semen Dezhnev's expedition along the coast of Siberia in 1648. The rumors first surfaced in 1779, when information about Kauwerak, an important Eskimo village on the Seward Peninsula, reached Siberia ("Kheuveren" is the Chukchi pronunciation of "Kauwerak"), and fanciful imaginations—which I documented in my article—put the crew of the lost boat in Alaska, still identifiable as Russians after 130 years of Eskimo intermarriage! ("The Kheuveren Legend," 1976).

A favorite setting-the-record-straight project was my article about Sinrock Mary (Mary Antisarlook Andrewuk), who became the most famous Eskimo woman of her day after she had inherited a small herd of reindeer upon the death of her first husband, Antisarlook. Despite her fame, the true facts of her life were elusive. Most of what had been popularly known about her reindeer herd and her various activities was exaggerated. I went back to official reports and archival sources for the article, "Sinrock Mary: From Eskimo Wife to Reindeer Queen" (Ray 1983:117–40; 1984b).

Ever since the first explorers came to western Alaska in the latter part of the eighteenth century and the early nineteenth century, Eskimo life has been affected by European and American goods and ideas. The rate of change has varied from time to time, but two events in the recent past have been instrumental in propelling Eskimos rather precipitously into the social, economic, and cultural life of Alaska. The first was the "Equal Rights Bill" of 1945, which I have already mentioned; the second was the Alaska Native Claims Settlement Act of 1971, which provided for the establishment of thirteen Native corporations, granted title to 44 million acres of land, and awarded $962.5 million to the Native peoples of Alaska.

Although changes in the economic and political life of Alaska Natives have had the greatest publicity, changes in the Native art world, which involved a comparatively small percentage of people, are equally remarkable. When I arrived in Nome in 1945, merchants provided the major incentives for Eskimo art production. The only possible acclaim to Natives for their work in exhibition or competition was to be gained in the annual Northwest Alaska Fair, where artists could enter various ivory and sewing categories for prizes—as much as fifty cents for a first prize!

The first effort to help Native craftsmen and craftswomen in production and marketing throughout the United States was made in 1935, with the establishment of the U.S. Indian Arts and Crafts Board in Washington, D.C. Assistance was extended to Alaska when the board, with the cooperation of Virgil R. Farrell, supervisor of a new arts and crafts division of the Bureau of Indian Affairs in Juneau, created the Alaska Native Arts and Crafts clearing house (ANAC), a marketing organization. Native artisans throughout Alaska sent their products to ANAC for distribution, but in the Bering Strait area, most of the goods produced went directly to the local stores or were sold in King Island Village or at the Nome Skin Sewers Cooperative (see fig. 37 and pages 72–76).

In 1992 I wrote a paper, "Beyond Souvenirs," for the Bering-Chirikov conference in Anchorage, in which I had the opportunity to discuss changes over time in Alaskan Native handicrafts since Alaska's official discovery in 1741, with a special emphasis on the forty-five-year period I had personally observed. In discussing the various projects, organizations, and programs that have benefited Native artists in recent years, I emphasized what they did *not* have when I begin my research. This bears repeating:

> Nowadays Alaska is awash in Native arts. It is difficult to imagine
> what a comparatively bleak artistic landscape it was in the 1940s and
> 1950s. Today, encouragement and financial support are given to all of
> the arts, including Eskimo art, by a multitude of organizations never
> dreamed of in those days. For example, there was no National Endow-
> ment for the Arts; no Alaska State Council on the Arts; no Percent for
> Art Program; no Alaska Contemporary Art Bank; no Visual Arts Cen-
> ter; no Festival of Native Arts; no program of Native art studies at the
> University of Alaska Fairbanks; and no Institute of Alaska Native Arts.
> There were no workshops, demonstrations, conferences, artists' resi-
> dencies, apprentice programs, or museum projects that hundreds of
> Alaskan Natives have been a part of during the past twenty-five years.
> No Native Alaskan artist had as yet received a college degree in art.
> (Ray 1992:370)[8]

Since the early 1970s there has been a blizzard of publications on
all aspects of Alaskan Aleut and Eskimo arts, including sculpture,
woodworking, basketry, beadwork, ivory carving, fur work, and
dolls. Through these publications, as well as catalogs of exhibitions,
the Eskimo artist has become well known, even famous, beyond
Alaska and is no longer the anonymous, almost invisible person of
the early years.

Contemporary Graphics

Throughout the years I have collected and given away (or saved for future gifts!) many original prints and drawings by Eskimo artists. I have bought them not only for their esthetic appeal but, at times, for their cultural and historical importance. Some are not "good art," but they provided a little cash for the artist. There are, of course, gaps in my collection, mainly because I was not in the right place at the right time. For example, I missed out on the works of Florence Nupok Malewotkuk and George Ahgupuk, although I eventually was able to get two very small Ahgupuk drawings when I visited him in Anchorage in 1976. There is, however, in this collection a rare portfolio of Ahgupuk's paintings, issued by Deers Press of Seattle in 1953, which was given to me in 1964 by Rachel Simmet of Anchorage, a serious collector of Eskimo art, who permitted me to study and photograph her collection.

The Professional Artists

Making a living as a professional artist began for the Eskimos with George Ahgupuk (illus. 1), although Happy Jack had succeeded as an ivory artist before 1918, but most of the ivory art was part-time work until the 1960s, when a few carvers devoted full time as prices for their objects increased. Ahgupuk's success in the new medium of paper drawing and painting was followed shortly by that of his brother-in-law, Kivetoruk Moses, as well as Robert Mayokok,

Florence Malewotkuk, and Wilbur Walluk. Howard Rock, founder of the *Tundra Times,* should fit in here, too, because he was the first Alaskan Eskimo to study art in a university setting, but he found it difficult to sustain a living as an artist (see pp. 149–51).

It is not surprising that the artists became so successful in a foreign medium, because missions and schools had lent their ideas and materials for decades before the 1930s and 1940s, when the new graphic art became popular. It is more surprising that commercialization did not begin sooner. Almost all of the schools provided drawing lessons, and teachers invariably remarked about their pupils' natural aptitude for art. But the success and fame of the artists from the 1930s on began with the publicity given by artist Rockwell Kent to Ahgupuk. In 1937, on his return from an Alaskan trip, Kent's articles appeared in the *New York Times* and *Time* magazine. The stage was set for a long line of Alaskan graphic artists.

Illus. 1. George Ahgupuk

George Aden Ahgupuk (figures 1–3)

Two artists, George Aden Ahgupuk of Shishmaref and Anchorage, and his brother-in-law, Kivetoruk Moses of Shishmaref and Nome, together have produced more drawings and paintings that depict the realities of Eskimo life and the romance of folktales than any other Alaskan artists. They have no equals as interpreters of their culture in graphic form.

Although Ahgupuk's career as a professional artist did not begin until 1937, when he was twenty-six years old, he had always liked to draw. During several months in the hospital in Kotzebue in 1934, recovering from surgery for a leg broken several years before, he had time for art. With the little money he earned selling his drawings, he realized the potential of pen and charcoal. As the story goes, on his return home to Shishmaref, he asked his mother for sealskins to draw on because he did not have any paper. The rest is history. His innovative use of this material brought fame and fortune to Ahgupuk.

He began sending his sketches to Nome for sale in 1935, and some were bought by Rockwell Kent. One of these, a square of sealskin entitled *Into the Corral* (part of a larger work), was published with an article about Ahgupuk in the *New York Times* for 11 January 1937. The article began:

> American art has encompassed a new and broader horizon with the
> discovery of a first-rate Alaskan Eskimo artist, according to Rockwell

Fig. 1. George Ahgupuk, Shishmaref. Page 1 from a portfolio of 18 black and white reproductions on paper. Deers Press, Seattle. 1953. 8½" by 12"

Kent. . . . There arrived in New York yesterday some examples of the work by his "find," whom Mr. Kent . . . describes as "unique . . . an original artistic talent, arising spontaneously, without suggestion or nurture, to meet the emotional and practical needs of an individual."

Although Ahgupuk's fame centered mainly around his sealskin panels, he also had a prodigious output on paper. He drew or painted many pictures for various publications. In the latter 1930s and early 1940s, he illustrated Christmas cards in color which were sold by the American Artists Group (New York) at the urging of Rockwell Kent. In 1945 he made India ink drawings for thirty-four folktales collected by Edward L. Keithahn, and in 1959 he illustrated the book, *I am Eskimo—Aknik my Name,* by Paul Green (Keithahn 1945; Green 1959).

Ahgupuk's most unusual publication, however, is the portfolio in this collection (fig. 1), which was published by Deers Press of Seattle in 1953, and entitled *18 Reproductions of Paintings by Alaska's Most*

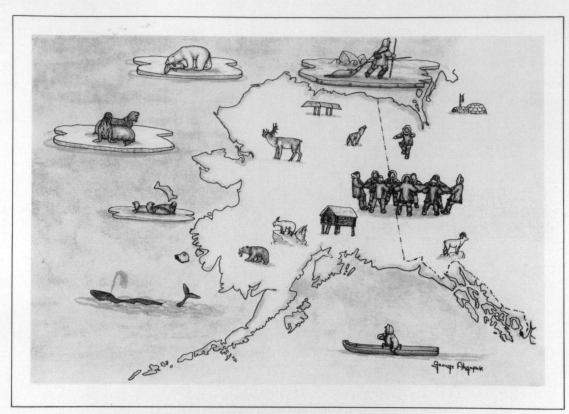

This is our Eskimo World . . . It is our native home . . . The great place called Alaska!

Distinguished Artist George Ahgupuk. The drawings, which are on separate sheets "so they may be pinned up, matted or framed," depict
the history of Alaska from the Eskimo viewpoint, all with descrip-
tive captions (figs. 1, 2, 3).

The first drawing is a self-portrait. The second drawing, the first in
the "history" series, is an outline map of Alaska with various Eskimo
scenes: "This is our Eskimo World . . . " The third picture depicts
birds, ice, bears, and a whale: "In the beginning, there were only the
sky, the water and Alaska. . . . " The fourth picture shows an umiak
under sail: "From across the waters came the Eskimo . . . " The fifth
is a dog team: "The Eskimos hunted in the hills . . . " From the sixth
through the eighth illustrations, the scenes depict the development
of traditional Eskimo life, but in the ninth appears a sailing ship:
"Then came the white men. . . . " The tenth through the fifteenth
are drawings of gold mining and of new people arriving to build
trading posts, missions, schools, and bigger towns. Soldiers arrive
during World War II. Ahgupuk's captions are as remarkable as the

Fig. 2. George Ahgupuk, Shishmaref. "This is our Eskimo
World." Page 2 of a portfolio of
black and white reproductions
on paper. Deers Press, Seattle.
1953. 8½" by 12"

Our people were pleased. They liked nice homes like the white man. They paid for them with skins, furs and fish. In these new houses babies played and were well. In the old barabaras many got sick and died.

Fig. 3. George Ahgupuk, Shish-maref. "Our people were pleased." Page 17 of a portfolio of black and white reproductions on paper. Deers Press, Seattle. 1953. 8½" by 12"

drawings themselves. They provide in a nutshell his perception of changes in Alaska:

10. [A prospector panning for gold]: Later other white men came with shovels and pans. They scratched in creeks for yellow pebbles. When they found them they shouted. Women came running, hugging and kissing. They cried, "More, more."

11. [A town of log cabins]: Then came other people. They hurried to Alaska like ducks and geese. Villages grew from trees. They built trading posts that sold all things for gold or money—things the Eskimos had never seen.

12. [People walking to a school where an American flag is flying]: "Some men brought preaching books. They built houses with steeples and bells. Other men brought reading and writing books and built houses with smaller bells. Eskimo children learned to read and write and sing "America."

13. [A town on a waterfront with saloons, stores, and a sternwheel

boat]: Villages grew bigger and spread out over the land. Where men found more yellow pebbles they made more towns and more stores. Big boats ran up and down the rivers. White women and children came too.

14. [Soldiers, airplanes, and an airfield]: "Then came men called soldiers—as many as the stars. They carried guns. Pretty soon the Eskimos were soldiers too. They lived in the white man's army houses and learned to march and salute.

The final four illustrations bring Alaska firmly into the twentieth century:

15. [Airplanes, ships, a train, men walking, and a highway with a sign, "Alaska," and a truck "Alaska or Bust"]: After the war people came like a big flood. They came to all the towns and in between. They came so fast there were many more people than houses to sleep in. But they didn't stop coming.

16. [Piles of lumber and ships]: Everything came to Alaska for building lots and lots of houses. They came for the Alaska Housing Authority. Lumber for white men's houses. Lumber for houses in Eskimo villages, too.

17. [An Eskimo family walks on a road, which has an old village of semisubterranean houses on the left, and a village of western-style houses on the right]: Our people were pleased. They liked nice homes like the white man. They paid for them with skins, furs and fish. In these new houses babies played and were well. In the old barabaras many got sick and died.

Ahgupuk's final drawing in this series (18) is his dream vision of tall buildings nestled high in a huge bank of clouds. Beneath this apparition travels a man and his dog team on the ice: "Eskimos now look at the big houses that birds must fly around. All they can say is 'Ah-yaaa, ah-yaaa.' There are no words in Eskimo to mean the big things the white man builds out of his head in Alaska." It did not take many years for this dream to materialize. Another artist, Robert Mayokok, wrote to me on 12 March 1965 that, in the year he had been gone from Anchorage, "Big buildings have sprung up. . . . Skyscrapers are standing out above the low buildings."

Kivetoruk Moses (figures 4–7)

I cannot think of Kivetoruk Moses apart from his wife, Bessie, who seemed to me to be his left hand while his right hand painted (illus. 2). Besides ordering his supplies, keeping their accounts, sometimes serving as translator, and answering letters, she often wrote a little description to go with his paintings, which usually told a story. I met them first in 1955, when he was still known in Nome as "James," and then again in 1964 and 1976, but especially in 1968, when he was so flooded with orders that he, too, like Mrs. Hazel Omwari, had to ration his paintings to his customers (see page 64). Everyone in Nome called them by their first names—it was almost unheard of to say Mr. or Mrs. Moses!

Kivetoruk was born in 1900 at Okevok near Cape Espenberg. He took his father's name of Kivetoruk as his artist name. Like George Ahgupuk, Bessie's brother, he found an early liking for drawing in the little schooling that he had, but he quit before he had finished the third grade because he had to herd reindeer and hunt and fish for his family. After he was injured in an airplane accident in 1953, he told me, he "took the art work and try to learn it again."

By the 1960s he had developed his distinctive style of bold India ink outlines and infinite shadings with colored pencils and water-colors. One of the outstanding features of his paintings is his metic-

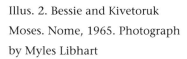

Illus. 2. Bessie and Kivetoruk Moses. Nome, 1965. Photograph by Myles Libhart

ulous, almost finicky, rendering of the sky, with its subtle coloring and cloud formations. Another is his attention to the smallest detail in every part of a painting.

He made duplicates of many of his drawings, but I do not think that he made duplicates of the pair in this collection (figs. 4, 5), which he named *Mr. Big Chief Navasuk* and *Big Chief Wife Mrs. Navasuk*. He painted these portraits especially for Alaska's centennial celebration in 1967. Kivetoruk's details are almost photographic: hair and eyebrows, ears, the woman's chin tattoos, the designs on their clothing, her earrings, and his tiny pipe that smokes a pinch at a time. Behind each portrait is one of Kivetoruk's dainty skyscapes, but Mrs. Navasuk's sky is more subdued than her husband's.

For her age and the limited advantages that were available to her, Bessie was a well-educated woman, which was evident in her business dealings and her command of the English language. She told me that Kivetoruk always gave her five dollars when she wrote an explanation or a story behind a painting that he sold. She wrote the

Fig. 4. Kivetoruk Moses, Shishmaref. *Mr. Big Chief Navasuk.* India ink, watercolor, and photographic coloring pencil on paper. Painted especially for Alaska's centennial year. 1967. 12½″ by 8¾″

Fig. 5. Kivetoruk Moses, Shishmaref. *Big Chief Wife Mrs. Navasuk.* India ink, watercolor, and photographic pencil on paper. Companion painting to *Mr. Big Chief Navasuk.* 1967. 12½″ by 8¾″

story of *Navasuk, North East Cape Siberian Chief, 1909* in blue ink on lined paper as follows:

> This true story is the 1967 Centennial celebration picture of the chief and his wife from Siberia.
>
> Every spring Navasuk the chief from N.E. Cape Siberia he send whole family to go trade for him through St. Lawrence, King Island, Big and Little Diomede Island and Wales then on up to Kotzebue.
>
> His sister and his oldest daughter are the part owners with him selling deer skin, deer legs, sinew, wolf skins and wolverines which they traded for all kind of Arctic skins caught during the Winter.
>
> They also sold Russian steel saw what make in ooloos and skin needles, tea, sugar and mostly tobacco which was the main reason our Eskimo waited for them every summer.
>
> Navasuk was the best hunter and had his own store and couldn't make the trip himself, according to people who goes there from here he own one of the biggest store.
>
> Even though they were enemies before they became good friends after one of the Chief married an Eskimo woman till trading was cut off by both our government and their government.
>
> Navasuk the chief and greatest hunter was killed by snow slide through witch doctoring by one of certain tribes there in Siberia.

Kivetoruk told me that his inspiration for *The First Airplane to Point Hope* was a postcard, and that a man named Assasuk, who had witnessed the flight, told him that the people in the umiak under sail were frightened to see the strange machine (a biplane) come suddenly out of the clouds (fig. 6). Two people in the umiak are bent over in prayer, and the man in the bow is reaching in supplication toward the airplane, but the man at the rudder calmly keeps the umiak on a steady course. From Kivetoruk's careful drawing, one can see exactly how a sail was rigged on an umiak. I asked him why he used yellow cardboard for this picture, thinking he may have wanted heightened drama, but he said that his order of white paper had not arrived, and since someone had given him this "yellow stuff," he decided to use it. He said that this was the first one of this scene that he had made, but he expected to do several more.

Kivetoruk painted several pictures with himself as the subject, most of them small, like *Reindeer Man, Kivetoruk Moses, age 21* (fig. 7). This is Kivetoruk, standing on the runners of his freight sled, which is pulled by just one reindeer. Again, he has given special attention to the technical aspects of the harness and line

Fig. 6. Kivetoruk Moses, Shishmaref. *The First Airplane to Point Hope*. India ink on watercolor and paper. The men are praying because they see a strange object in the clouds. 1968. 10″ by 15½″

Fig. 7. Kivetoruk Moses, Shishmaref. *Reindeer Man, Kivetoruk Moses, age 21*. India ink and photographic coloring pencil on paper. 1968. 4¾″ by 11″

attachments. Even though there is a bank of clouds in the sky, one sees that the day is bright because the sled, the dog, and the reindeer throw faint shadows on the snow.

I shall always remember Kivetoruk not only for his exquisite paintings but for his unfailing sense of humor. One day I stopped by his house while he was at work painting, seated at a table. I asked if I could buy four or five of his most expensive pictures, although he had told me he was rationing his works. He dropped his little brush, squinted up at me, and said, "Dorothy, I think you some kind of millionaire!"

Robert Mayokok (figures 8, 9)

Robert Mayokok was an illustrator in the best sense of the word. His economical line-drawings of the entire range of Eskimo activities were used in many ways: as drawings to be mounted for display, for greeting cards, on pottery and dishes, on gift-wrapping paper and bags, and as illustrations in books, some of which he wrote himself. Robert was called both "Robert" and "Mayokok," but his closest friends and peers always called him "Robert." When I first met him in 1950 in Nome, where he had gone to recuperate from his first bout with tuberculosis, I asked him how he pronounced his name, and he answered, "Any way you like!"

Robert Mayokok (illus. 3) was born in Wales, Alaska, in 1903 and died in Anchorage in February 1983. Like Arthur Nagozruk, Charles Menadelook, and Billy Komonaseak, who are mentioned in the discussion about Komonaseak's cribbage board (fig. 59), Robert reaped the benefits of the legacy of a good school program begun by William Thomas (Tom) Lopp and Harrison Thornton in 1890. This, combined with a talent for both art and languages, made him unique among the early graphic artists. In my long association with him I was amazed at his fluency in, and colloquial use of, the English language and his constant searching for the most appropriate words and correct grammatical constructions. His five booklets (see References) are in precise English, and, based on the many letters I received from him, I am sure that the printers did not change the text in any way.[1]

Illus. 3. Robert Mayokok

Robert gave me the box in this collection in 1968 when I visited him in Anchorage (fig. 8). I had not seen a box like this before, but I think he made drawings on more boxes after that. This was a small, readymade box on which he drew the following scenes with a felt-tip pen: the sides featured a dancing group, a polar bear on an ice

Fig. 8. Robert Mayokok, Wales.
Trinket box. Wood with India
ink drawings on sides and top.
1968. Height: 3⁵⁄₁₆″

floe, a hunter spearing a seal, and a bear killing a seal. The lid
depicted a man dragging a seal.

The 1984 calendar (fig. 9) issued by the Easter Seal Society of
Alaska, features thirteen of Robert's drawings, made in 1980. He had
donated these drawings, and many others over the years, to be used
as fund raisers for the society. In October 1982, according to a brief
essay in the calendar, the society voted "to establish The Robert
Mayokok Scholarship Fund through the University of Alaska Foundation, to provide scholarships for handicapped art students at our
state schools." Funds for the scholarship were to be provided
through the sale of the calendar.

The drawings range through all subjects of Eskimo life—ice fishing, bear hunting, seal hunting, blanket tossing, dancing, reindeer
herding, and drawings of various animals—but the two most interesting are his interpretation of Noah's Ark, on the cover, with its
imaginative array of animals and people, and the illustration for September, which shows five panels of vigorous subsistence activities.

NOAH'S ARK

9-12-80 Robert Mayokok

Fig. 9. Robert Mayokok, Wales. *Noah's Ark.* Cover of Easter Seal Society of Alaska calendar. India ink on paper. 1984. 8½" by 11"

His letters outline the progress of his career in the graphic arts, from its beginning in the Seward sanatorium (as well as during the two years he spent at the Riverton Sanatorium in Seattle in 1954–56, after a relapse) where, he wrote, "I took to drawing pictures depicting Eskimo life and writing small booklets on primitive Eskimo. . . . I have never taken art lessons, except about 4 hours in water colors. I use oils on canvas and velvet. [He also used reindeer, sealskin, and rabbit skin.] Most of my work is with pen and ink. I do etching on ivory with hand engraver. All of my artistic interest was started when recovering from surgery at the hospitals where I spent five years [three years at Seward; two years at Riverton] as T. B. patient" (Mayokok to author, 12 February 1968).

Mayokok took a no-nonsense approach to his art because he suspected that other artists were thought to be better than he, but he was proud that he had been able to find his way in the new foreign culture with dignity and a measure of happiness through his art. He closed his eyes to slights that he sometimes felt; for example, the time that he was passed over for a spot in the Manpower Development and Training Act program in Nome in 1964–65, because the people in charge did not like his art.

Between his release from the Seward hospital in 1950 and his admittance to Riverton in 1954, he tried a number of jobs—radio broadcasting, selling carved ivory as a middleman, and experimenting with oils—but always drawing. Just before he left for Seattle, he painted three large oil paintings (3 by 4 feet) for Wien Alaska Airlines to pay for transportation between Fairbanks and Barrow, where he had stayed for two weeks. He also "made a deal with them" to paint three more the same size for transportation to Kotzebue, so that he could take photographs. He was also painting on velveteen, a material that he considered to be "fascinating" because, with the right application, he said, the paint could make images look three-dimensional. At that time he also had letterheads printed with his drawings (Mayokok to author, 29 September 1954).

By the early 1960s, his tuberculosis cured, he traveled to several cities as far south as San Francisco to show a film he had made of Eskimo life, but his art was still his primary concern at this time. Yet he was unable to live comfortably on his art income alone, so in January 1962, when he was asked to clerk in a new gift shop that specialized in Native products, he accepted. Also, he said, "You know I like to meet people." The job did not last long, however, because the owner went "Outside" with all the money and left Robert stranded (Mayokok to author, 2 January 1962).

Although Robert was best known for his pen-and-ink sketches— and indeed they were the backbone of his income—oil painting fascinated him. In 1964, just before the devastating Good Friday earthquake, he had hung a number of oils at the Book Cache. In his letter of 29 March he wrote: "I just heard interviews over the radio [that] it was just about a total loss. So, I guess I lost several hundred dollars worth of pictures. That represented several months of work. It won't be easy for me for a long time. . . . I guess I was lucky to get away with my life."

With his stock depleted and business poor, he took a job at an Alaskan exhibit at the New York World's Fair in 1964 for a steady income. He stuck it out to the end, although he was stifled in the city, and the people he worked for went back on many terms of his contract. After a difficult winter that included gallbladder surgery, he took the job again during the summer of 1965. However, he had had a display of his works at The Eskimo Shop during the Fur Rendezvous in the spring (Mayokok to author, 25 January and

12 February 1965).

On his return to Anchorage in early 1966, his career took off in many directions, so much so that he wrote: "There is so much to do I don't know where to start." He had an order of 200 drawings for a bank; he was asked by Tony Bockstahler of Alaska Woodcraft in Eagle River to draw on wood plaques; he had a request to illustrate a children's book and also to illustrate an album and booklet of music and folktales (Mayokok to author, 24 March 1966; see also Caswell 1968; Koranda 1972).

But another event that year set his career on the path that never deviated until his death, as he became essentially an "artist-in-residence," first at the Gilded Cage Gift Shop and later at the Alaska Treasure Shop.[2] When he was asked to open a studio at the Gilded Cage, the Crippled Children's gift shop, he accepted. He said, "it will be a good place to meet people," and meeting people was one of life's pleasures for this outgoing man. He stayed at the Gilded Cage until 1 September 1968, when he and the manager, Bill Sain, moved over to the Alaska Treasure Shop. There, over the years, Robert chatted with hundreds, maybe thousands, of tourists and let them watch him at work. But before he left the Gilded Cage, he had designed a gift wrapper and paper bags, had completed some panels of small story pictures, and had begun painting on ceramics in addition to sealskin. He was also "doing some soapstone sculpture [from] soapstone near Palmer area. Very unique in color. Gray in natural appearance, changes color when varnish is applied to speckled jade-like color and black." And then, finally, he was "doing some oils for a change. Doing pen sketches becomes monotonous especially after doing four hundred individual pieces." (Mayokok to author, 25 March, 10 June, and 20 September 1967)

He wrote to me that there was "lots of competition in the Art field. Lots of good Artists in Alaska. I mean real Artists—not abstractionists. Machetanz is one of the best." (Robert had told me years before that he was the model for the young hunter in Fred Machetanz's lithograph, *The Hunt,* which had also been reproduced as a holiday greeting card in the 1950s.) He named the "Eskimo artists" in 1968: "George Ahgupuk, Wilbur Walluk, James Moses Kivitoruk [Kivetoruk], John Oakie, Jr., and Florence Malewoktuk [Malewotkuk] are the most outstanding." He did not include himself!

Bernard Tuglamena Katexac (figures 10–22)

Bernard Tuglamena Katexac (illus. 4) grew up on King Island. Because of its isolation, his village held on to its old ways longer than most Eskimo villages, except possibly those of southwest Alaska or Little Diomede Island. Katexac lived the same subsistence lifestyle as his fellow artists during his youth, but he arrived at an artistic eminence by quite a different route because, unlike them, he received formal art training at the University of Alaska Fairbanks, graduating with an Associate of Arts degree in printmaking in 1966.

I had known Bernard since my earliest days in Nome and had an off-and-on correspondence with him, especially in 1970 and 1971, when it seemed that we might collaborate on his biography. He and I were contemporaries—he was born in 1922—and we always met each other on a friendly, yet formal, basis. When I last saw him in 1986 he was almost incapacitated. He was living at the Nome hospital, but he wanted me to help him rearrange his art supplies at the XYZ Club (the senior center). He could not really work at his art—perhaps the materials in the small room provided for him were there merely to hold on to the past.

Bernard's career began during a six-weeks' pilot program carried out in Nome in 1963 by the University of Alaska Fairbanks as a

Illus. 4. Bernard Tuglamena Katexac in the print-making studio. 1965. University of Alaska Fairbanks, 1965

"study to determine improved methods and changes needed to increase and expand the market for Alaska native arts and crafts" (University of Alaska, 1964, p. 1. The project is summarized on pages 134–44 of the Report). This experimental workshop, which preceded the MDTA Designer-Craftsman Training Project of 1964–65 (in which thirty-two Eskimo trainees became acquainted with new equipment, materials, and designs for contemporary markets), was open to everyone regardless of ethnic origin, but of the fifteen students enrolled, only three were Eskimos. Bernard was one of them. The workshop stressed theory of design and innovation, and many participants dropped out. Although it was advertised for anyone to join, it actually had been organized only for *Native* craftsmen. The contract stipulated that "if persons of outstanding ability are discovered, up to three of these people will be offered a scholarship [not called a 'grant . . . in order to avoid difficulties in complying with regulations of the Internal Revenue Service and the University covering special students'] . . . to the University of Alaska for up to one (1) academic year, in order that (a) their response to traditional art and design training on the crafts work of other craftsmen of their respective villages can be learned" (ibid.:134, 142).

Up to this time Bernard, at forty-one years of age, had been a hunter and an ivory carver, providing for his parents and going to Nome during the summer with the other King Islanders to live in King Island Village. The report of this experimental workshop said that Bernard was "selected because he is a carver of recognized ability and because of his desire to do something more with himself and his talents. An autobiography which he wrote while at the University [his first year there, 1963–64] indicated a long felt desire to work in other media . . . but a hopeless feeling as to how to break out of his environment." He returned to King Island for hunting and sketching at the end of the 1964 academic year and planned to open a studio in Nome, but he was advised to return for another year at the university, which he did. While at the university he had formal training in many aspects of art: sculpture, oil painting, metal work, and especially printmaking, for which he was widely known. He continued his printmaking until the early 1980s, when he became ill.

The etching entitled *Tutut* (caribou) in figure 10 is one of his best works. It was chosen by Saradell Ard, the artist and specialist in Eskimo art, to be included in the 1982 *Inua* exhibit of E. W. Nelson's collection at the Smithsonian Institution, and in the subsequent publication (Frederick 1982: fig. 337). *Tutut,* a large etching with a powerful image of mountains and snow, combines the strength and delicacy, the shadows and light of both the land and the caribou. The caribou look dainty as individuals but are an immense force as a group. The blackness of the mountains contrasts with the snow, and one of the most dramatic parts of the etching is the huge herd of caribou moving down the steep snow-covered hill from light into shadow, while several single caribou emerge from shadow into light in the foreground, the antlers of the two leading caribou dramatically black against the snowfield on which the main herd is descending.

When I was in Nome in 1968, Bernard and I discussed writing his biography. For several years we had a brief correspondence trying to coordinate visits and interviews, but it never happened. He kept saying in his letters that he was "thinking" about writing biographical notes, but at the same time he wrote about current events such as one busy day in the summer of 1970, when, after a six-days' walrus-hunting trip around King Island, he returned to Nome and "spent most of time reading some of my art books and trying to think how I can make another picture—carve ivory—drink beer and now I have two linoleum blocks all ready for a try-out and still have another in mind for a woodcut and a big tusk all set to polish for a cribbage board and still have to work on either same size or smaller one and a wolf mask to work on for an order and still have another printing to do for a friend in the Fish and Game and one more print of the 'KIUVOKMIUT II' the final and send it with the block to a museum in Anchorage." As for the biography, "I don't even know where to begin. . . . It's like when I'm about to study in a college without taking any high school graduation" (Katexac to author, 28 July 1970).

Earlier that year he had been in Seattle, where he had been given the use of a studio. I was in Washington, D.C., so our discussions about a biography and about prints that I wanted to buy were carried on long distance. It was at this time that he made the woodcut prints, *Shadows in a Pond* (fig. 11) and *Old Ivory Etchings* (fig. 12), which are in this collection. On 30 March 1970, he wrote that he had almost finished his "new composition, Shadows in a Pond," from an idea that had come to him when a friend "turned on *music* in his car as I felt the music in a metropolitan air from a quiet place. There is a swan, a goose in background and carved ivory bird in middle like a ptarmigan. Hoped it will come out a proof as I'm working much more carefully. The smaller plates I had long ago most of them destroyed, so I had to substitute almost all of the

Fig. 10. Bernard Tuglamena Katexac, King Island. *Tutut* (caribou). Engraving, artist's proof. 1964. 17⅞" by 11¾"

2/50 SHADOWS IN A POND   Bernard Katnoe - 70

works with new larger ones. I like to work larger—now I might work smaller so people can afford to buy them."[3]

On April 14 he wrote that he had sent ten copies of *Old Ivory Etchings* to Juneau, and that he would print one for me. He said that *Shadows in a Pond* still seemed "poor to me. I think I need another

Fig. 11. Bernard Tuglamena
Katexac, King Island. *Shadows in
a Pond*. Woodcut in color. 1970.
18" by 11½"

Fig. 12. Bernard Tuglamena
Katexac, King Island. *Old Ivory
Etchings*. Woodcut. 1970.
11½" by 24½"

blue so my subjects could show better." He intended to send both to
a gallery, but "only if SHADOWS IN POND come out as I like (I'm
ashamed of it) [will I] be sending them to you." He also said that he
"had in mind to carve a plate about a girl with a shee fish [he did],
darn thing I have been forgotten my small sketch book in Nome.
And since Nome has been quite excited when musk oxen was trans-
planted in the area last month, I've drawn some here and it's a problem for me to place them in a plate how to arrange them for a
composition [he made this one, too]. I might get to Fairbanks some-
day so sometimes I think to print a racer with hair flying around the
head with sign overhead, 'ANUAL FAI' and if the picture come [out]
I would put in the title, 'Go Rhonda go.'"

After 1971 he continued his printmaking with a brief stint at the
new Visual Arts Center in 1974, and he demonstrated printmaking
at the Arctic Arts Festival in Anchorage. He occasionally carved
masks and engraved ivory on order. He also designed logos for
advertisements, a memorable one being a pouncing eagle for Foster
Aviation in Nome in 1973. Although he could say in a rare
depressed moment that "some day I will just eat seals and spider
crabs and walrus, never mind prints" (Katexac to author, 30 March
1970), I think that he had never lost the longing to return to

6/15 AVIK   Bernard J Katexac —63

college, which had been one of the high points of his life. In 1971, after a brief illness and under medication, he wrote me from Nome that "if I'm fit for it I might find out I'll be able to go back to college to work toward trying to get a BA degree" (Katexac to author, 23 July 1971). He never did go back, but he had more than fulfilled expectations as the first participant in the Native arts program at the University of Alaska.

Bernard Katexac's unique talent, transformed from that of an ivory carver in a fairly isolated milieu into a sophisticated print-maker, is a watershed in the history of Alaskan Eskimo art. The thirteen prints in this collection show the breadth of his subject matter and technical mastery during his most productive years. In addition to the 1970s prints just discussed, there are three made in 1963—*Avik* (fig. 13), *Nanuk Niak Toac* (fig. 14), and *Woman Skinning Seal* (fig. 15); five prints from 1966—*Cutting Walrus Hide* (fig. 16), *Cutting Whale* (fig. 17), *Tufted Puffins* (fig. 18), *Walrus and Calf* (fig. 19), and *Woman and Child* (fig. 20); the 1972 *Girl with a Sheefish* (fig. 21); and the 1974 *One Chance* (fig. 22).

Fig. 13. Bernard Tuglamena Katexac, King Island. *Avik*. Woodcut in color. 1963. 4¼" by 5½"

Fig. 14. Bernard Tuglamena Katexac, King Island. *Nanuk Niak Toac*. Woodcut in color. 1963. 10″ by 8¾″

Fig. 15. Bernard Tuglamena Katexac, King Island. *Woman Skinning Seal*. Woodcut in color. 1963.

25/46 CUTTING WALRUS HIDE — Bernard Katexac -66

8/35 CUTTING WHALE — Bernard Katexac -66

Fig. 16. Bernard Tuglamena Katexac, King Island. *Cutting Walrus Hide.* Woodcut in color. 1966. 4¾" by 7½"

Fig. 17. Bernard Tuglamena Katexac, King Island. *Cutting Whale.* Woodcut in color. 1966. 6" by 6½"

Fig. 18. Bernard Tuglamena
Katexac, King Island. *Tufted
Puffins.* Woodcut in color. 1966.
5½″ by 6″

Fig. 19. Bernard Tuglamena
Katexac, King Island. *Walrus and
Calf.* Woodcut in color. 1966.
4¾″ by 5½″

Fig. 20. Bernard Tuglamena Katexac, King Island. *Woman and Child.* Woodcut in color. 1966. 8" by 6"

Fig. 21. Bernard Tuglamena Katexac, King Island. *Girl with a Sheefish.* Woodcut in color. 1972. 17" by 7½"

Fig. 22. Bernard Tuglamena
Katexac, King Island. *One
Chance*. Woodcut in color. 1974.
10½″ diameter

Peter J. Seeganna, (figures 23, 24)

Peter J. Seeganna (illus. 5) was a talented printmaker as well as an ivory carver and wood sculptor, but when he returned to Nome from the Indian Arts and Crafts Board workshop in Sitka in 1968, he did not have facilities for printing. He continued, however, with his wood sculpture. And, of course, he was busy with the management of Sunarit Associates, a Native business, which I discuss later in connection with his wooden walrus (fig. 44).

Both *Cormorant* and *Survival* are examples of the new approach to art by the artists of Seeganna's generation, and they show the benefits of formal training. *Cormorant* (fig. 23) is a rather somber abstract rendition of a bird in brown, black, and white. *Survival* (fig. 24) is his interpretation in blue and gray of the ribbon seal and the spotted seal, the basic animals for food, clothes, and utensils.

Peter Seeganna and Bernard Katexac studied art at the same time, but Bernard chose to follow the path of a more representational art

Illus. 5. Peter J. Seeganna

Fig. 23. Peter J. Seeganna, King Island. *Cormorant.* Woodcut in color. 1967. 10¼" by 15½"

Fig. 24. Peter J. Seeganna, King Island. *Survival.* Woodcut in color. 1967. 6½" by 11⅙"

than did Peter. Both, however, diverged from the pictorial representation of Ahgupuk, Mayokok, and Moses. Along with several of their contemporaries, especially Joseph Senungetuk, Seeganna and Katexac changed "Eskimo art" to the wider world of "art."

Inupiaq Picture Writing

During an interview for the *Fairbanks Daily News-Miner* in May 1993, I was asked to name my favorite research project. I had not been told beforehand what questions would be asked, but the answer I gave on the spur of the moment—of all the many possibilities in my research into Eskimo history and the arts—is the same one I would give today: the recording of the picture writing used by the Inupiaq people for remembering the Scriptures. This small project was not an integral part of my larger projects, but I had the fun of playing detective in a mystery that had the right ending, with the satisfaction of rescuing an almost forgotten part of Inupiaq history.

In 1954 I first encountered the picture writing used by people living in Buckland and Kotzebue when I read *Alaska Natives,* by H. Dewey Anderson and Walter C. Eells. The authors compared the Buckland and Kotzebue versions in two Bible verses with pictographs, English verse, and Eskimo translation, but they did not explain why a particular picture or symbol was used. For example, the meaning for the English word "I" was evident from the stick figure of a person. But why was a symbol that looked like the letter "U" with a circle on the tip ends used for the word "truth?" (Anderson and Eells 1935:191). But it appeared that my curiosity had reached a dead end, with no hope of pursuing the matter, because the authors twenty years earlier had reported that picture writing was almost a thing of the past at the time of their research in 1930 and 1931 (ibid.:190).

But in 1964 fate stepped in when I met Lily Ekak Savok, a missionary of the Covenant Church (illus. 6). I discovered that she had been one of the inventors of the picture writing! At one time picture writing had extended all the way from Kotzebue Sound as far south as Koyuk on Norton Bay. Unfortunately Lily and I met at the end of the summer, and I had to return home. But in 1968, with the help of her daughter, Ruth Outwater, and her daughter-in-law, Gladys Saccheus Savok, I was able to learn from her the meanings behind the symbols used. I had hoped to obtain more examples, but Lily was recovering from a stroke at age seventy-five (she died in January 1980), and the work was tiring for her because she insisted on my getting "everything right."

Ruth Ekak: Picture Writing (1920s) (figure 25)

Lily, who was born in 1893 to Egak (Ekak) and Koliraq of Buckland, told me that her mother (given the Christian name of "Ruth") had invented the picture writing with her help so that the older Eskimos who could not read English could remember the Scriptures. Many people in the Kotzebue area had quickly adopted Christianity, and her family had been one of the earliest members of the California Yearly Meeting Society of Friends, which was established in Kotzebue in the summer of 1897. Nevertheless, Lily's father moved the family from their Buckland River home to Unalakleet, so that Lily, at age seven, could go to school at the Swedish Covenant mission. Lily, whose Eskimo name was Tusagovik, was precocious. She soon became so fluent in English that she served as an interpreter when

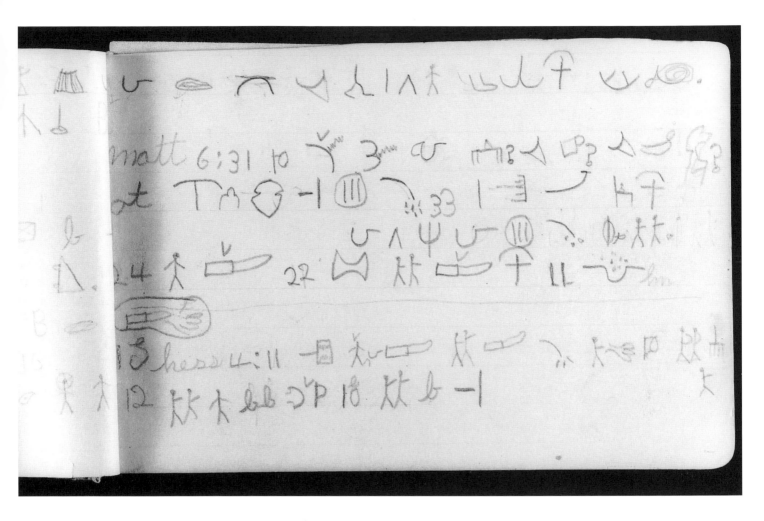

Fig. 25. Ruth Ekak, Buckland. A page from her practice notebook of picture writing to remember the Scriptures. Pencil on paper. 1920s. 4½" by 6¼"

Illus. 6. Lily Ekak Savok explaining Eskimo picture writing to author, Kotzebue, 1968. Photograph by Jim Richardson

quite young. As we worked on the verses, Lily told me that I was taking her back more than fifty years, when she began drawing her first pictures so that her father, who did not speak English, could remember the verses.

The Ekaks' picture writing was not the first that had been devised in Alaska for the Scriptures and hymns. The first was a remarkable picture writing invented by Uyakok ("Helper Neck"), a Kuskokwim man born between 1866 and 1870 in the village later called Akiachak. (This is the village from which Aleš Hrdlička took several memorial posts. See page 87.) He gradually developed his pictographs into a syllabic writing system that did not employ pictures, after he became a "helper" in the Moravian church beginning in 1892. In time his writing developed to the point whereby he was able to indicate every syllable. (A summary of Helper Neck's life and orthography is given in Henkelman and Vitt 1985:355–73.) An example of his mature writing is in one of his Bibles in the Archives,

University of Alaska Fairbanks.[4] After I had published an article about the Buckland picture writing in *The Beaver* (1971a), I learned about Alfred Schmitt's 1930s study of the Kuskokwim pictographs and orthography which was published in 1951. Schmitt gave a number of examples in pictographs and Yup'ik and German languages, but he explained very few of the symbols (Schmitt 1951).

I asked Lily if she had seen the Kuskokwim picture writing, but she replied that she did not know what it was. She was born a few years after Helper Neck had begun working with the Moravians, so her mother would have been Neck's contemporary, although the date of her birth is unknown. The picture writing seems to have been independently invented, but there are striking coincidences in the lives of Neck and the Ekaks. Both came from families with shamanistic backgrounds. Neck, before his conversion to Christianity, and his father were shamans, and Ruth Ekak's father had been a "strong" shaman in the Buckland area. Spiritual concerns continued into the next generations. Lily and her husband John Savok became missionaries, first for the Friends at Kotzebue from 1910 to 1948, and then for the Covenant church, as did their son, Fred. With his wife, Gladys, Fred presented the "Eskimo Hour" on the church's KICY radio station in the 1960s. Neck's legacy also continued through one of his sons, Lloyd Neck, who became the first Yup'ik man to be ordained as a Moravian minister in 1946 (Henkelman and Vitt 1985:372).

Working with Lily Savok was a wonderful adventure into the uses of imagination and poetry as applied to a pragmatic situation. Her long life as a missionary, explaining to her people the basics of Christianity, made her an eloquent speaker of English. The verses of Philippians 4:4–7, were Lily's favorites. She wrote these as well as many others in both Inupiaq and English for me, drawing the symbols as she explained why they were used (Ray 1971a; Ray 1983: 141–48). (See Appendix, p.170, for illustration.)

Katherine Toots: Picture Writing (1950s) (figure 26)

In 1976, when I visited Nunivak Island, I added a postscript to the Inupiaq picture writing—a surprise in the Yup'ik area. I was given a faded page from an old, lined notebook with the hymn, "On Zion's Hill," sketched in pictographs by Katherine Toots. The meanings were explained for me by Hilma Shavings. I have included this fragile page in this collection. The pictographs and meanings resemble the Buckland writing, as well they should, because the picture writ-

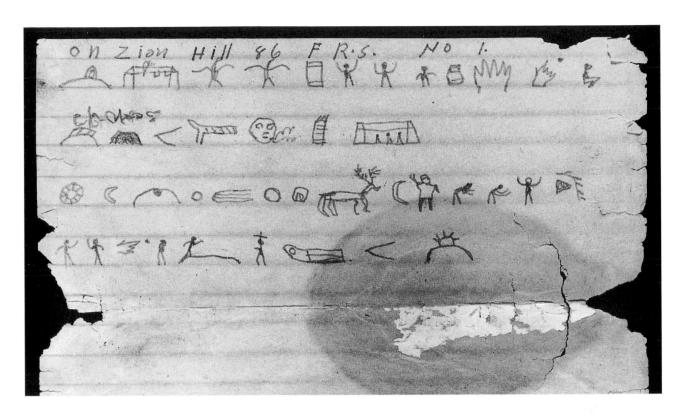

Fig. 26. Katherine Toots, Nunivak Island. "On Zion's Hill," three verses and a chorus of a hymn in picture writing. Pencil on paper. 1950s. 9¼" by 7¾"

In 1976, Hilma Shavings of Nunivak Island explained this example to me, verse by verse, image by image, as follows, with tracing from original picture writing:

1. *On Zion's Hill* (a hill) *a mansion stands* (a house) *for all* (loons, which mean "all" because loon means the same in Eskimo) *the pure* (towel, "to clean") *and blest* (two men are "blest"). *We know it was not made* (small man and a "something made" object) *with hands* (first hand). *Up there* (hand pointing up, and a dot means "there") *the soul may rest* (man sitting).

Chorus: *On Zion's blessed hill* (two hills) *the soul's eternal* (a V on its side, "the ends go on forever") *home; God's voice* (face speaking) *is softly calling still* ("perhaps something at rest, standing still") *to rest beneath that dome* (house with people in it).

2. *No sun or moon is shining there* (a sun, a moon, and a dome with a dot inside—"not shining—hiding") *to light the streets of gold* (a circle for a light; lines for the street; and coins, i.e., "gold"). *The Lamb's* (a reindeer) *own light* (a moon, "because light sounds like moon in Eskimo") *so wondrous fair* (a person with raised hand) *the saints* (figures in supplication) *with joy* (arms upraised) *behold* (an eye).

3. *To meet you* (people) *there* (hand and a dot, "not up, but there") *I mean to live* (a person) *while here on earth I stay* (a man on a line representing the ground). *There Christ* (figure with cross on his head) *a welcome* (a kayak bow, "to welcome; when come by kayak to a strange place, are pulled up to shore by the hole, and welcomed") *sweet will give for one eternal* ("the ends go on forever") *day* (sunrise).

ing was brought to Nunivak Island by Swedish Covenant missionary Jacob Kenick, whom I had visited one sunny day in 1968 at his fairy-tale wooded camp near Shaktoolik. Kenick was born in Golovin in 1886 and had gone to Nunivak Island in 1932 as a missionary with his first wife, Sarah Amigitchoak.[5] After she died, he married a Nunivak Island woman, Edna, who learned the picture writing from him.

In 1950, L. L. Hammerich, a Danish linguist, purchased a manuscript of Edna Kenick's picture writing. He gave the original to a Danish museum, and a copy to the University of Alaska Fairbanks in 1970. In 1977 this Nunivak picture writing was published in Denmark with two forewords, one by Robert Petersen, who said that Edna Kenick had developed her pictorial writing from Helper Neck's. This is not true. Mr. Petersen apparently was not aware of the northern picture writing on which Mrs. Kenick's writing was based, and he jumped to the conclusion that she had copied it from Neck, who died in 1924. Although the "handwriting" of the pictures is slightly different from the Ekaks' (it varied from person to person), it is definitely in the northern style and bears only a generic resemblance to that of Neck (Hammerich 1977).

Mainly Women's Work

Several pieces in my collection bear witness to the ingenuity with which the women have applied their traditional skills to the making of marketable objects. Under the heading of "women's work," I include examples of coiled basketry techniques, skin sewing, and soft-bodied doll making.

Coiled Grass Basketry and the Coiling Technique

A well-made coiled grass basket (fig. 27A) only two inches high has had a special place in my collection because it is a reminder of a basketry tradition that was abandoned in the Bering Strait area after the 1918 influenza epidemic. The survivors turned their talents thereafter to sewing furs to make a little money. When I first lived in Nome, in 1945, there was only a handful of baskets for sale, all of which were imported from Stebbins, northwest of St. Michael. (Most of the Stebbins people at that time had come from Hooper Bay.) The only others for sale in Nome were baleen (whalebone) baskets, made in Point Hope and Barrow, and a few birch bark baskets from the Kotzebue area.

I acquired this basket in 1963 from the family who had bought it in Nome in 1902. At one time four little ivory seals, carved in the old blocky style, were attached to the sides, but one was now missing. A piece of thread on the lid also gave evidence that a finial, possibly of ivory, had once been attached. I took the basket to a veteran

Illus. 7. "Eskimo Hand-made Baskets, Teller Alaska." Photograph by F. H. Nowell, 1904. Carrie M. McLain Memorial Museum, Nome, neg. no. 83-1-209

carver, who readily made a copy of the old-fashioned seal for the side, but he insisted on making a sleek, up-to-date (i.e., "realistic") seal for the lid. The little seals proved to be quite different from attachments on most early Bering Strait coiled baskets, which were unadorned for the most part. Occasionally, a tuft of fur or a simple design of beads were attached, almost as if by afterthought, which detracted from rather than added to the artistic worth of the basket. Ivory attachments are rare on grass baskets, except for an occasional finial, but a coiled basket in the Sainsbury collection at the University of East Anglia, England, is similar to this one, only in larger size (9½ inches high), with eight ivory seals attached around the largest circumference of the basket, and six lozenge-shape ivory figures attached in a circle on the lid (UEA 696).

Early gold-rush observers had scarcely anything to say about basketry—their silence is as if there had been no basket making—but those zealous photographers, B. B. Dobbs and F. H. Nowell, have recorded what was apparently a thriving occupation for the women at Bering Strait (illus. 7). Prior to the gold rush of 1900 at Nome, Miner Bruce obtained a number of baskets from the Kotzebue Sound and Teller areas which were deposited in the Field Museum in Chicago. The seven baskets from Port Clarence and the three collected at Kotzebue Sound were probably made for household use, not as souvenirs; for example, one oval basket, from Kotzebue Sound, 6⅝ inches long, without a lid, was used to store personal possessions, and the smaller baskets held sewing materials when women prepared skins outdoors. A basket maker worked part time for three days to make the large basket. Although they are well made, they do not have the finish and precision of those sold in the Nome and Teller areas a few years later (VanStone 1976:25, 48–50 passim, and pl. 22; and VanStone 1980:50–51 and pls. 24, 25).

It is ironic that the best coiled baskets at the turn of the century were made by Inupiaq basket makers in the Bering Strait area, where none is made today, while world-famous baskets now come from the Yup'ik weavers in southwest Alaska, where, until the 1920s and 1930s, basketry was uneven in construction and uninteresting in design.

The origin of the coiling technique is unknown.[1] I know of only a few pieces found in archeological sites, and their age is problematical. As Otis Mason wrote, in his 1904 study of aboriginal basketry: on the basis of baskets in the Smithsonian Institution (some collected by E. W. Nelson), "it is quite certain that the art of basket making is not an old one with these people [the Eskimo about Norton Sound]. . . . It must be admitted, however, under the stimulus and demands of trade, that the art is improving. Specimens are at this date brought home that are vastly better made than any of the old pieces in the National Museum" (p. 400).

Small Coiled Basket (figure 27)

The small basket in this collection (Nome, 1902, fig. 27A) certainly bears this out. It is well made and sturdy, with very fine coils, especially on the lid. The largest coil is 0.24 inches wide, and the smallest, only 0.08 inches. Unlike the older ones in the Smithsonian which were started on the bottom with a piece of hide or left open (because, as Mason wrote, "they have not learned how to begin the work from the center of the foundation"—ibid.), this tiny basket was started with the 0.08 inch coil. There are eight coils on the bottom, which measures only 2 inches wide.

Grass basketry from southwest Alaska, in villages like Hooper Bay, Kongiganak, Mekoryuk, Tununak, and Newtok, might be called "late bloomers" because their ascendancy as an art form is only about two generations old. Margaret Lantis, ethnographer of the Nunivak Island people, has said that women there did not make coiled basketry until the 1920s, when a trader introduced the coiling technique (Lantis 1950). Clark M. Garber, superintendent of the Yukon-Kuskokwim school district in 1932, reported that "some art baskets have been wove . . . for sale to the white traders but now the traders have ceased to buy them. At Tanunak and Pastolik the native women have acquired a considerable skill in the making of art baskets, but since the demand for their products died, there is no inducement for them to continue the manufacture" (Garber 1932:6).

Basketry has now become an elegant product; shapes are symmetrically perfect and the women's imagination has soared beyond the earlier attachments of beads, fur, or tufts of yarn in geometric designs to include almost anything the weaver wants to portray, sometimes with a whimsy that is rarely seen in Eskimo art. Some of the subjects depicted on recent basketry are a man fishing through the ice near his sled, birds, a man pulling a seal, butterflies, an exotic animal leaping among flowers, and snowmobiles (illustrated in Ray 1981: figs. 87–91). Coiled basketry also has become the basis for unusual shapes: plaques with imbricated human and animal figures, "yo-yos", dolls, crustaceans, masks, and even a kerosene lamp (see fig. 28; also see illustrations in Ray 1981: figs. 75, 82, 83, 94, and 95).

Large Coiled Basket and Coiled Mat (figure 27)

When I bought this large basket (fig. 27B) in 1960 from Arctic Traders, Inc., based in Seattle, I was appalled at the price (less than $10), not because it was high, but because it was so low. Before the merchant's markup and transportation costs from a remote village, the basket maker was probably paid only pennies for her work. During my study of the ivory carvers in Nome in 1955, we (the carvers and I) figured that they were making only a dollar an hour, but "throwing in" the ivory for free! Perhaps this basket maker from Scammon Bay made ten cents an hour at the most.

Since this favorite basket was on display in our house for many years, the little geese, which were dyed red, purple, and blue, have faded, although I remember that even at the beginning they were not as vivid as figures on similar baskets.

Fig. 27. A: Anonymous, Nome. Miniature coiled grass basket with ivory seals attached. 1902. Height 2"; B: Anonymous, Scammon Bay. Basket. Coiled grass basketry with color imbrication. 1960. Height 13". Circumference 49"; C: Anonymous, Stebbins. Hot-dish mat. Coiled grass basketry. About 1940. Diameter 14¼"

Women from Stebbins were known in the 1940s for their trays and hot-plate mats. During the early part of the twentieth century, a few Hooper Bay families moved to Stebbins and brought with them their coiled basketry tradition. Most of the mats averaged about 7½ inches in diameter, so this one (fig. 27C), which is 14½ inches in diameter, is unusually large. The rose, tan, and purple-black colors on the "right side" of the mat are somewhat sun-faded. They are not faded on the underside, where some of the coils are uneven and the wrapping is erratic.

Susie Chanigkak: Coiled Basketry Lamp (figure 28)

Nowadays certain baskets are noted for their enormous size, or for their exceedingly small size, or for their unusual beauty, but, whatever the attributes, no piece of basketry has given me more pleasure to look at or to think about than the coiled basketry replica of a kerosene lamp illustrated in figure 28. The kerosene lamp, which replaced the traditional seal oil lamp, is now superseded by the electric light bulb in all but the most remote areas of Alaska. I wish that I could have asked Susie Chanigkak of Kongiganak, who made this piece in 1976, why she chose to coil into sculpture an everyday object rather than a doll or an animal with a more conventional "artistic" character. A basket maker has to have unusual proficiency in the coiling technique to make a piece like this, and an innovative imagination as well to transform a glass and metal object into a unique piece of basketry sculpture.

The lamp is made in three parts: the chimney; the wick section, with the wick turner placed exactly right; and the base, which is ornamented with grass dyed purple and green.

Objects fashioned in the shape of non-Native tools and utensils are not new in Alaska. Women of all Native groups have tried their hand at imitating western objects in basketry. Tlingit women made many objects in twined basketry before the turn of the century, and they made even more after tourists began going to that part of Alaska. I have seen cups, platters, sugar bowls, pitchers, and tureens made of willow root by Athabascan women. Eskimo women have been just as prolific, making a range of objects that include an alarm clock (the old-fashioned kind with a bell top) and a basket made in the shape of a crustacean from Nunivak Island. The body of this unusual basket has two long feelers and six legs made of coiling, and it comes alive on the lid with eyes and a skeletal design sewed on with blue and red raffia (see Ray 1981: fig. 83).

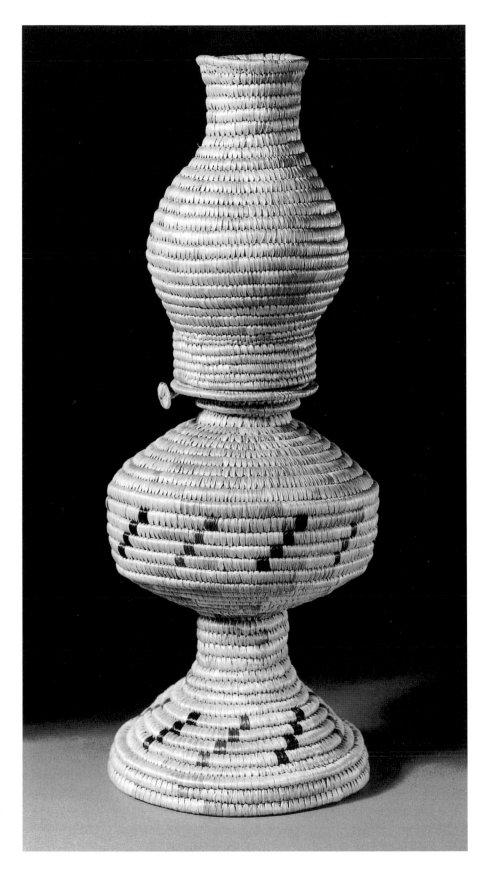

Fig. 28. Susie Chanigkak, Kongi-
ganak. Replica of kerosene lamp.
Coiled grass basketry. 1976.
Height 14″

Viva Wesley: Coiled Basketry Doll (figure 29)

Once the Nunivak Island women began using the coiling technique, their talents bloomed, and, contrary to custom, they borrowed pictorial designs that had previously been the prerogative of the men. At the same time, they invented geometric designs in appealing

Fig. 29. Viva Wesley, Mekoryuk, Nunivak Island. Doll. Coiled grass basketry with fur accessories. 1978. Height 7½"

arrangements, which, according to Lantis—at the time she was writing in 1950—buyers preferred to the naturalistic figures "sometimes slapped helter-skelter on the sides and tops of the baskets." (Lantis 1950:71)

By the 1970s their work was more uniform, and they had even begun making dolls by coiling. The doll in figure 29 was made by Viva Wesley of Mekoryuk on Nunivak Island in 1978. Ethel Montgomery, who was a long-time employee of Alaska Native Arts and Crafts in Juneau, told me that grass dolls did not appear for sale until 1975, when Hooper Bay women began to make them. However, since the Nunivak women were coiling in other shapes before 1941 (see, for example, a crustacean, Lantis 1950:68) it is possible that dolls dated before 1975. Mrs. Montgomery added, however, that in 1949 she had seen two grass dolls that were sent to the East Coast, but no others had come to ANAC until the 1970s. This doll, 7½ inches tall, is made entirely of grass, even the face and legs as well as the small round mat on which it is mounted. The doll wears a hat and mittens made of ground-squirrel fur, white calfskin, otter, and seal. The eyes are blue beads under purple raffia eyebrows. A purple grass ball hangs from a necklace made of blue and white seed beads. The dish or hat at its feet is of the same color as the ball.

Skin Sewing: Dolls, Appliqué, Parkas

The making of ivory and wood dolls in earlier times was the province of the men, but when Americans and Europeans arrived in Alaska, the women turned their sewing abilities to making soft-bodied dolls. The women of every village have made dolls of every available material: fur, tanned skin, gutskin, cloth, and, as we have seen, even basketry. Dolls are always dressed in the style of parka, pants, and boots worn by the sewer herself, or in the style of her village. Like basket makers, doll makers have usually been anonymous, but in recent years a few doll makers have become known by name. For example, Dolly Spencer, formerly of Kotzebue, has become renowned for her dolls that resemble real people. These dolls sell for thousands of dollars. Most customers, of course, pay considerably less for dolls that many women make in their spare time. These buyers are content to own a doll that is simply "an Eskimo in a parka," as a reminder not only of Eskimo life but of the doll maker herself.

Hazel Omwari: Doll and Dancers (figures 30, 31)

The doll and plaque in figures 30 and 31 were made by Hazel Omwari of St. Lawrence Island in 1968, while she was living temporarily in Nome as an outpatient at the hospital. Between medical appointments, she sewed dolls and dressed them in contemporary colorful cloth parkas, and she made wall plaques of drummers and dancers appliquéd on a fur background of light-colored hair seal.

Although the doll is dressed in a cloth parka typical of parkas throughout the Bering Strait area, it is identifiable as a St. Lawrence Island doll by the fur ruff, the fur around the face, and the amulet belt of tanned sealskin under the parka. The torso, arms, and legs (under the parka) are sewn of figured cloth with lavender, orange, and white flowers on a green background; the cloth cap, which is removable and ties under the chin, is made from the same fabric. The parka's figured cloth has a design of tiny red and yellow flowers on a black background and is trimmed with yellow rickrack. As an example of Mrs. Omwari's meticulous work, both the inside of the parka hood and the ruff itself are neatly lined with cloth. The face is made of tanned sealskin, with embroidered features and black plush hair. The doll wears red diapers. She has no feet or hands, just like my old favorite rag doll.

The appliquéd plaque (fig. 31) is a piece of cardboard faced with hair seal and backed with a linenlike cloth. A half-moon piece of ivory is attached to the top as a hanger. Eight cut-out figures (three drummers and five dancers) are attached to the seal fur with minute stitches. Mrs. Omwari cut the figures from her own patterns and backed them with tissue to make them appear three-dimensional. The making of scenes and activities with cut-out figures for wall hangings, pillows, and even parka trim originated in the 1950s with the women of the Nome area, especially those who attended the Covenant church, but it was Mrs. Omwari's innovation to use tissue behind the figures.

The tallest dancer is 2½ inches high and the seated drummers are 1⅝ inches high. Two of the three drummers wear fur coats—one white and the other brown—but the third man wears a pure white parka of tanned sealskin. The drums and sticks are also made of tanned sealskin. Two of the dancers wear parkas of fur—one is white and one is gray, almost the same color as the background fur. The other three parkas are of tanned and dyed sealskin, two are red and one is aqua-blue. All of the dancers wear mittens—such tiny things

Fig. 31. Hazel Omwari, St. Lawrence Island. Plaque. Dancers of dyed seal parchment attached to backing of seal fur. 1968. 9½″ by 7½″

to be sewn to the sealskin! All wear Eskimo boots, which are commonly called mukluks throughout the Bering Strait area.

That summer (1968) I wanted to buy several dolls and plaques, but Mrs. Omwari's work was so popular that she had to ration it. She explained apologetically that I could have only one of each because she could not show favoritism to any of her customers! Somewhat as consolation, though, she let me buy two unmounted figures—a dancer, and a woman with a child astride her shoulders—which she was planning to use in a new scene.

Margaret Johnsson: Doll Parka and Felt Appliqué
(figures 32, 33)

The doll parka made of sealskin in figure 32 is an example of the finest sewing done by an Eskimo seamstress. Few can equal the fur sewing of Margaret Johnsson, who made this parka for a large doll in 1966. (I shall say more about Mrs. Johnsson as a young girl, when she was a participant in the Inviting-In Feast of 1912. See pages 87–90.)

I met Mrs. Johnsson in the 1960s, first in her home in Mukilteo, Washington, and later in Edmonds, where I often visited her on my way to or from Seattle and Port Townsend on the Edmonds-Kingston ferry run across Puget Sound (illus. 8). She always had a treat for me—canned king salmon, white muktuk (from beluga whale), and dried or smoked salmon strips. She was always busy sewing. I never saw her without a piece of fur or cloth in her hands.

Margaret Johnsson was born in 1897 in Unalakleet of an Unalit (Yup'ik) mother and a white father, Maurice Johnson, who deserted his family of two children when she was a baby. She did not lose contact with him, however, and she had a number of his possessions, including a brief account that he wrote of his adventures as a census taker in 1900. On one of my visits, she asked me if I thought it interesting enough for publication. Having a look at it, I decided that it was suitable for the *Alaska Sportsman*. It was published in the October 1968 issue, titled "Taking the Census in 1900," and Margaret was so pleased to see it in print that she gave me the little parka as a gift.

Margaret was famous for her felt appliqué pictures of Eskimo activities (fig. 33); for her full-size "fancy parkas"; and for her doll parkas, which were always 18½ inches long. By 1971 she had made twelve full-size parkas as well as eight other doll parkas similar to this one she gave to me. She also made many parkas, mukluks, mittens, and hats for her family while living in Alaska, before she and her husband, Eric Johnsson, a dog musher and U.S. Marshal, retired in 1959 to a warmer climate. She made her first doll parka in 1932 for a daughter who died young. Margaret later gave that parka to the University of Alaska Museum. She sold a doll parka to the U.S. Indian Arts and Crafts Board in the 1960s, and gave the rest to her grandchildren.

Margaret had wanted to make this parka of ground-squirrel fur, like her first one, but she was unable to get the skins in 1966. Today, in the 1990s, squirrel skins are almost a thing of the past, since few

Illus. 8. Margaret Johnsson in her home. Edmonds, Washington. 1974. Photograph by author

Fig. 32. Margaret Johnsson, Unalakleet. Doll parka. Sealskin with trim and insets of calfskin. 1966. Length 18½"

Fig. 33. Margaret Johnsson, Unalakleet. Eskimo scene. Felt appliqué and embroidery on fabric. 1960s. 16" by 20"

people take the time any more to snare squirrels. Even in the 1960s, women (who were the principal squirrel hunters) snared them only to provide skins for their own sewing, and they rarely had skins to sell.

This parka is made principally of sealskin, with front shoulder insets. The back of the hood is made of white calfskin. The ruff is wolf. Decorative strips of wolverine fur hang from horizontal strips of plucked beaver in two places, both front and back. Above each beaver strip are three strips of calfskin—a strip of white on each side of a black strip—each strip only ⅜ inches wide and 1⅜ inches long. Six small red beads are sewn onto each bottom white strip. This same motif of parallel strips and beads is placed just below the shoulder on each sleeve, and extends in a continuous design, front and back, in a strip about 3⅞ inches long with nineteen red beads.

On the back of the hood, the same configuration edges the white calfskin, with eighty-four red beads on the outer white strip, and runs in a continuous line from bottom to top, around the top, and to the bottom of the opposite side. The trim at the bottom is also a three-part design, but larger, with a middle part made of alternating white and brown calfskin strips, and finished at the bottom with a pinked strip of red flannel.

The parka is lined with blue and white cotton and has a zipper, so the parka can easily be put on a doll.

The use of imported calfskin, especially for trim and sometimes even for an entire parka or pair of boots, had been popular for many years when Mrs. Johnsson made this doll. But in traditional days, white caribou calfskin had been used. Before domesticated reindeer (a relative of the caribou) were introduced into Alaska, the white in clothing was a touch of conspicuous consumption, because at that time the only white on clothing was obtained from the rare Siberian reindeer with white spots. This was a costly trade item which only the richest Eskimos could afford.

Lucy Berry: Activity Dolls (figures 34–36)

In the latter 1960s I became aware of a new trend in doll making: Eskimo women were making dolls that were *doing* things—everything from women dancing to men pulling fish from a hole in the ice. I do not know who made the first one, or in what village, nor do I know who devised the name "activity doll," but most that I have seen were made by Yup'ik women of southwest Alaska, although a few Inupiaq women also made them.

The six dolls in this collection were made about 1972 by Lucy Berry of Napakiak, a village about fourteen miles downstream of Bethel at the mouth of Johnson River, which empties into the Kuskokwim. I did not know Lucy Berry. I bought the dolls from a woman in Sequim, Washington, who had once lived on the Kuskokwim, where she had become acquainted with the people, but she did not give me any information about Mrs. Berry.

I have seen other activity dolls in exhibits and illustrated in articles, but none of Mrs. Berry's dolls. Yet she portrayed a wide range of activities and had a knack of suggesting, in the frozen moment of sculpture, the vitality of the person in a specific activity. The faces and hands of the dolls are made of a commercial plastic fabric, and all wear well-made mukluks and cloth parkas, which are called *kuspuks* among the Yup'ik speakers.[2] All of the dolls' *kuspuks* are made

Fig. 34. Lucy Berry, Napakiak. Activity dolls. A: Man cutting seal meat (7¼"); B: Man making a net (5½"). Cloth, fur ruffs, metal, string, wooden bases. 1972

from various cotton materials: the women wear patterned cloth, but the two men (one is cutting up seal meat, and the other is making a net) wear solid color parkas (fig. 34). The net maker (who is old, since he has pure white hair!), wears a white parka; the seal cutter, one of red corduroy with an aqua-blue rickrack design. All but one of the parka hoods have fur ruffs, but three of the figures are bare headed, with their parka hoods thrown back off their heads. All hoods are anchored in place and cannot be moved.

It is difficult to choose a favorite among these six dolls, since each depicts a different activity, but two that stand out are the "storyknife" dolls and the nurse's aide. Telling a story and illustrating it in mud or snow with conventionalized drawings in a set order with a storyknife was a favorite pastime of Yup'ik girls in southwest Alaska. They used an implement of scimitar shape, from four to

twelve inches long, made of bone, antler, ivory, or even wood. Ivory was the overwhelming favorite, because it could be ornamented in many ways by the male relative who made it for the girl. The game apparently has a long history. Archeologist Wendell Oswalt found storyknives in an excavation dating from A.D. 1690 at Hooper Bay, and E. W. Nelson collected many from various villages in 1880. The handles of some of these were decorated with bas-relief circles, geometric designs, and bird beaks. This pastime was "performance art" in its purest form, a unique three-way combination of storytelling and drawing with the storyknife, itself a piece of sculpture, as the story progressed in its set order, changing with each stroke of the knife (Ray 1981:44–45).

In Mrs. Berry's depiction of the storyknife performance (fig. 35), one girl holds a storyknife (made of wood) which she has just used

Fig. 35. Lucy Berry, Napakiak. Activity dolls. Storytelling with a storyknife. Cloth, fur ruffs, wooden base. 1972. Doll on right: 6″

Fig. 36. Lucy Berry, Napakiak. Activity dolls. A: Woman making Eskimo ice cream (5″); B: Nurse's aide (9½″); C: Woman making a grass mat (4⅞″). Cloth, fur ruffs, yarn, metal, twine, rye grass, wooden bases. 1972

to make a square (for a house) in the mud to begin her story, while the other girl sits comfortably on a log, gesturing with her left hand. Cotton surrounds the mud to represent snow on the wood base, and a bit of reality is provided by the dead moss that peeps up at the edge of the mud near the girl sitting on the log.

The woman identified as a village nursing aide strikes a nice modern note. She holds "A Nurse's Book" under her left arm and a medical bag in her right hand as she starts out on her winter rounds in the snow, a parka hood on her head, and tall fur boots on her feet (fig. 36B). Somehow, the *kuspuk* cloth of green leaves and blue flowers on a tan background seems appropriate for this serious young woman.

The other figures also have details that identify their activities: Mrs. Berry has woven cotton string for the net maker's net (fig. 34B) and coiled grass for the mat maker (fig. 36C). She has used heavy metal for the seal cutter's ax handle and shallow pan (fig. 34A) which is full of minute chunks of wood for realistic looking "meat." She mixes tiny red beads with cotton in what appears to be a child's metal toy dish to represent the making of "Eskimo ice cream," a mixture of berries, snow, and oil (fig. 36A).

Ground-Squirrel Parka (figure 37)

This squirrel-skin parka was made by one of the members of the Nome Skin Sewers Cooperative Association in 1946. Called a "sports jacket," it departs from the traditional Inupiaq woman's *atigi* or *parky* (the usual pronunciation of "parka" in Alaska) in three ways: it is short, at hip length, rather than long; it is straight around the bottom-instead of being rounded front and back; and it has a front zipper—the older garments never opened in the front, even with buttons.

This parka, though only fifty years old, is already a treasure from an era that has passed. Few, if any, parkas are made of ground-squirrel fur in the 1990s. As we have already seen, Margaret Johnsson resorted to using sealskin for a doll parka in 1966 because of the scarcity of squirrel skins. Except in workshops that are reviving Eskimo sewing, few fur garments of any kind are made today, because down jackets and pants have supplanted furs for most cold-weather purposes.

This parka is 37 inches long from the tip of the hood to the bottom of the strip of geometric trim, which is made of "outside tanned" calfskin. The inside of the hood is lined with squirrel skins, and the rest of the parka, including the sleeves and back of the wolf ruff, is lined with a tan nylon fabric. Wolverine fur finishes off the sleeves and the bottom of the parka, which is still in fairly good shape, although I wore it constantly for several years in Nome and Fairbanks.

The Nome Skin Sewers Cooperative Association

The Nome Skin Sewers Cooperative Association was one of the first Native efforts in northwest Alaska to work as a group for the benefit of their own people. Although it was not formally organized until 1939, its roots were in the Native school of the 1920s. Two women who later became instrumental in founding the Cooperative, Mabel

Ramsey and Emma Willoya, were on the Native school board. When the question arose as to what work would most benefit the Eskimo pupils economically, the answer was classes in ivory carving and skin sewing. Looking back seventy years, this seems to be a narrow agenda, but the social and cultural climate then was one of segregation, uncertainty, and widespread discrimination—vastly different from the 1990s. In those days, carving and sewing were the mainstays of the Eskimo population living in Nome. The only alternatives, longshoring and a bit of work in the mines, were seasonal for just a small percentage of Eskimo men.

From the Native school sewing classes came the idea of a sewing cooperative, which simmered without much direction until an arts and crafts specialist from the Alaska Native Service came to lend a hand in 1934. They remained loosely organized until 1939, when they were asked to make clothing for Admiral Richard E. Byrd's expedition to the Antarctic. Not until after they pooled the bonuses that they received for this work did they form the Cooperative. Besides establishing an on-the-premises organization where orders for clothing could be filled by local sewers, and where consignments of goods could be sent by members living in outlying villages, the Cooperative was also envisioned as an association that could help with social services. All Eskimos could join, and the initial membership consisted of seventy-six members, twelve of them men. (I took these figures from a list made in 1940, but in a 1950 talk, arts-and-crafts specialist Leah Levers said that there were originally 133 members. I have been unable to verify this.)[3]

Members paid a one-dollar initiation fee and were required to buy at least one five-dollar share. Shares were to be cashed only at death, for a funeral, or if a real need arose (and then it was considered a loan). The minutes of the meetings that I read for the years 1948–50 had many references to the misuse of shares by members. The minutes also revealed that the organization had struggled to keep afloat and probably would have sunk several times had it not been for several devoted women who gave much beyond their necessary duties. Especially effective were Mabel Ramsey, who served as president of the membership for several years, and Emma Willoya, who became the manager (illus. 9). Emma had to contend with tardy orders, unpaid bills, unfair competition by white commercial stores, and, once, embezzlement (which the perpetrator afterward said was a "loan," although she had not applied for it beforehand).

The Cooperative had a number of customers in Alaska and in the lower states who could order from a small illustrated catalog and price list. Directions were given for measuring mittens, mukluks, slippers, and parkas. The kinds of furs available for parkas were also listed: "July reindeer fawn, squirrel skin, spotted hair seal, common hair seal, outside rabbit (spotted, white, tan, or gray), and muskrat," which was in limited supply. All of these furs had been tanned "Outside [in the lower states] . . . unless otherwise specified." The latter phrase meant "Native tanned," rarely used for commercial purposes. All parkas were hand-sewn of reindeer back sinew (or whale sinew, if they had no back sinew) and were made with a full-length zipper and double lining. Ruffs could be made of dark or light wolf, wolverine, or polar bear, and the hood could be unlined or, like this jacket, lined with fur. Designs of calfskin trim could be specially made.

I spent a lot of time throughout the years in the Skin Sewers building, sometimes to learn about the sewing, sometimes just to visit because it was generally a happy place. One day in October 1950 I had no sooner stepped in the door when Emma Willoya said that I had missed all of the excitement. "The place has been swarming with photographers, and we've had the place just stuffed full of people, and am I mad!" All of the sewers were "mad" because the photographers from the *Saturday Evening Post* magazine, who were illustrating an article by the writer Sally Carrighar, had demanded that they pose wearing fancy fur parkas while they sewed, and with babies on their backs. One young woman refused to go home to get her baby, and was the only one who did not wear a parka. "I was so mad," she said, "that I wouldn't put my parka on. Imagine having the picture taken with them sewing with their parkas on and the babies on their backs! We never do that! Now they'll probably put in [the article] that we stink, and that the room is so cold that we have to have our furs on to sew."

Emma was still manager of the Skin Sewers in 1955, but she was upset about conditions there, although she remained until the spring of 1960. In 1954 she finally took a five-month vacation (her first since 1940), only to return to find that "practically everything went to ruin." The books were not kept up to date, employees had been absent much of the time, and orders were not filled. Emma herself had to take garments home to sew at night. The arts and crafts specialist at that time had been of no help; as a matter of fact, Emma told me that "most of the arts and crafts people who are sent up here do not know anything about their crafts, and they come repeatedly to me to find out about it; yet they are sent here to supervise us."

Illus. 9. Emma Willoya in her fancy parka. Nome, 1950. Photograph by author

The Skin Sewers were still getting goods from the ANICA stores (Alaska Native Industries Cooperative Association, Inc.), but of late, she said, the villagers had other outlets. For example, the Wales people were selling mostly to the people working at the tin mines at Tin City, five miles southeast of Wales. By 1955 the rules had changed so that non-Cooperative members were permitted to sew. I do not know when the Cooperative completely disbanded—it was not operating in 1964—but it was very evident that Emma Willoya's leadership had been paramount in its success.

Wood

Except for masks, wood is not often thought of in conjunction with Eskimo art and manufactures. It was, however, a very important material for the people who lived on the coast where rivers deposited fallen trees. The farthest-north groups, at Point Hope and Barrow, were not as fortunate as those living farther south, some of whom reaped fabulous harvests of wood.

Manna from Upriver

Wood had numerous practical uses: in umiak, kayak, and house construction as well as in the making of a whole spectrum of household and subsistence utensils: dishes, spears, harpoons, bows and arrows, sleds, racks, caches, among many other things. Artists used wood for masks and many kinds of sculpture, and, among the Yup'ik, they painted wooden spoons, dishes, and bowls with unusual designs. The wood came like manna from up the river, and it might have been possible that an Eskimo who used wood in a dozen ways had never seen a living tree.

Ceremonial Spoon (figure 38)

The ceremonial spoon from the Kuskokwim River, with a mythological figure painted in black on the bowl, is probably as old as the earliest piece in the collection, the engraved snow beater (fig. 45), which dates from 1866. The fanciful depiction of a Yup'ik creature exemplifies the difference in graphic art between Yup'ik and Inupiaq speakers. Although the Yup'ik occasionally portrayed animals in realistic form in their old art, most of their graphic art, which was painted on bowls, boxes, spoons, ladles, drumheads, and even on masks and kayaks, was related to a wide range of mythological creatures. Their Inupiaq relatives farther north, on the other hand, were more realistic in their graphic art on ivory. They recorded everyday events in a more-or-less representational style, although their cosmos was filled with as many mythological beings as that of the Yup'ik.

Between 1877 and 1881, E. W. Nelson collected many wooden objects painted with mythological figures in southwest Alaska, and although he was unable to obtain their meanings, he illustrated them in his book, *The Eskimo About Bering Strait* (Nelson 1899:66–72, pls. xxix–xxxii). Many years later, in 1937, Hans Himmelheber obtained paintings on drumheads that illustrated stories told to him during his study of the artists on the Kuskokwim River and on Nunivak Island. Invariably, these were "ancestor-stories" of unusual events that had happened to a member of the family in years past, or were about mythological animals that the artist or an ancestor had encountered (Himmelheber 1993:16–23, 58–60).

Himmelheber did not describe the painting of wooden utensils except on one occasion, when wooden bowls were painted in conjunction with drumheads while the people were preparing for a festival on Nunivak Island (ibid.:68–72). (Drumheads were made of stretched walrus stomach and sometimes seal intestines. One drumhead—illustrated in Himmelheber's English translation with the caption: "The mother and the wolves"—is now in the University of Alaska Museum in Fairbanks. I illustrated it in *Aleut and Eskimo Art,* with the original caption translated from the German edition: "Dreadful experience of a widow with a pack of wolves"—Himmelheber 1993: illus. 15; Ray 1981:fig. 190). According to Himmelheber, the "scene-painting" was restricted to only "one part of the southwest area, namely from Kuskokwim to Nelson Island. Beyond that one finds only beginnings—some single animal on a drum—but no vivid scenes."[1]

This spoon (fig. 38) is painted with a wash of hematite in two shades of red. Four X's and the head and skeletal motif of the animal are painted with black paint, probably a mixture of coal and blood or urine. The phrase, "Kuskokwim River. Ceremonial spoon," in old-fashioned handwriting, is on the back of the spoon. I do not

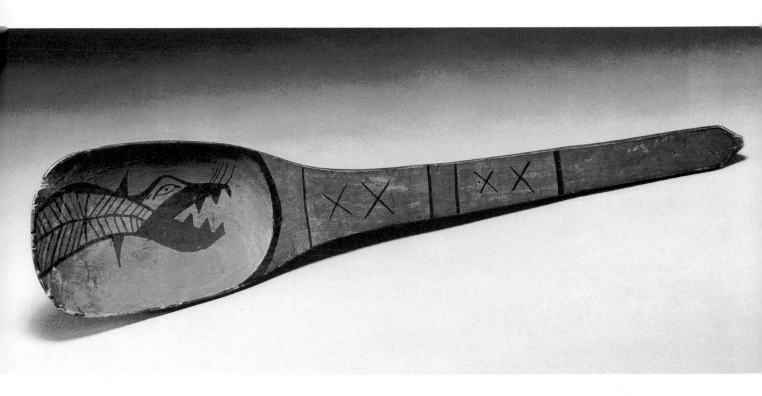

Fig. 38. Anonymous, Kuskokwim River. Spoon. Wood painted red; mythological figure in black. Nineteenth century. 17½"

know when the spoon was brought to Seattle, but I bought it in 1953 from Ye Olde Curiosity Shop on the Seattle waterfront as my first artifact purchase in Seattle.

Almost all of the painted figures on the spoons and dishes that Nelson collected appear to be of mythological creatures or fantastic beings of folklore; many show an interior view of the animal, as on this spoon. None, however, resembles this figure. One illustrated by Himmelheber—with the caption: "An ancestor found a dead white whale on the coast (Painter Timothy)"—is somewhat similar, although I suspect that the creature on this spoon is a different one altogether (Himmelheber 1993: no. 4).

This spoon seems to have been made for use despite the painted designs, and it probably has withstood innumerable immersions in liquid. Pigments were made to withstand such use by mixing the black or red colors with blood, according to Himmelheber, and indeed, I have seen bowls and spoons so dark with grease that I could scarcely see the designs. Nelson wrote that the black paint on a spoon from Chalitmut (on the mainland between Nunivak Island and Kuskokwim Bay) was still durable "although the utensil has been used in hot water and in greasy compounds" (1899:67).

Himmelheber's artists of Nunivak Island and the Kuskokwim River in the 1930s were still painting story representations from the past, but in the 1950s in the Bering Strait area, which was once the center of a unique graphic ivory art, the descendants of those talented engravers could not explain the scenes on the nineteenth-century bow drill handles (drill bows), although one man said that "a good guesser can guess exactly." Some of the people I talked to in the 1950s and the 1960s had never seen a drill bow with pictorial engraving, and no wonder, since all had been collected by the 1890s (see page 105). With new western-style tools the men no longer needed the bow drill. However, they turned their talents to the engraving of traditional themes, including mythological beings and ceremonial dancers, on large pipes, tusks, and cribbage boards. The Yup'ik painter, too, turned to the outside market, and subsequently made copies of old figures, or invented new ones, for sale.[2]

Bentwood Bucket (figure 39)

The Alaskan Eskimos made containers from a variety of materials—bags from animal skins of all kinds and salmon skin; baskets from beach grass; and dishes, boxes, and buckets from driftwood that came down the rivers to their beaches. Boxes ranged from tiny ones—in plain oval, round, or square shape, or in the likeness of an animal—made to hold arrow points, spear and harpoon points, snuff and tobacco, woman's implements, and miscellaneous trinkets, to large boxes in various shapes for tools, especially the long boxes made to hold a man's bow drill. The most elaborate boxes, usually carved from one piece of wood, were made by the Yup'ik people of southwest Alaska. The bentwood bucket, made of thin wood planks, was most popular in the area north of the Yukon River, especially in the Norton Sound area.

Buckets like this berry bucket, dating from the latter part of the nineteenth century in St. Michael, were made of planks that were bent under steam or in water into oval or round shape. The ends were sewn together with wet root, rawhide, or—as at Barrow— baleen. Bentwood containers were made in several sizes, but the large ones usually had a bail for carrying and were made for two different purposes. Household buckets, like figure 39, were made in traditional oval shape, and were usually colored red on the outside, with a beveled lip on the top inside, and a groove running around the top and bottom on the outside. In 1964 Simon Sagoonik, who was then past eighty years of age, told me that two-handled buckets, 2½ feet in diameter and 2 feet high, were made at Ayasayuk, the old village at Cape Nome, for storage of berries. The berries were

Fig. 39. Anonymous, St. Michael. Bucket, said to have been owned by Chief Tugalina. Wood. Late nineteenth century. Height 9½"

preserved dry (not with oil, when put into a seal poke). A skin cover was stretched over the top, and the bucket was set in a cold place.

The other kind of bentwood bucket was used only in whaling ceremonies and in the umiak while hunting whales. One of these buckets, with its charms and ivory handle with whale effigies, was found in 1912 on Sledge Island by a pupil from W. B. Van Valin's school at Sinuk, north of Nome. This is illustrated in the book *Raven's Journey* (Kaplan and Barsness 1986:144), as is a photograph made by Van Valin of a whaling ceremony, showing a bucket with ivory chains attached hanging from a pole. Michael Kazingnuk of Little Diomede

Island told me in 1955 that a whaling bucket absolutely had to have a chain attached to be effective for hunting whales.[3]

Few bentwood buckets like this one were collected when they were still in use, and few have been preserved. Perhaps they were never very common, or perhaps the people did not want to give up a useful utensil. I was told that making a bucket like this took a very long time in the old days. If they were rare even in traditional days, it explains why this bucket has been repeatedly repaired and treasured all these years.

I acquired this bucket in 1968 from Thora Katchatag when I stayed with her at her camp, Chauiyak, on the Unalakleet River. I do not recall the details of the transaction, and though she was not reluctant to part with it, she repeated several times that I was not to forget that it was "a berry bucket that had belonged to Tugalina, the last chief of St. Michael." Tugalina's name had surfaced several times when I was in St. Michael and Unalakleet, but I was unable to learn much about him. In St. Michael, Benjamin Atchik told me that he had been a famous caribou hunter, who slept out in the hills while hunting. Known as a generous and hospitable man, Tugalina brought caribou home to feed the people. When visitors came from Unalakleet, and other villages farther north, he saw to their wants, but he was a stern host, telling them "what to do, and they obeyed him."

It is not surprising that the bucket was made from an imperfect piece of wood having two knotholes, one of which still has a wooden plug in it, because Tugalina probably did not have any other choice. The supply of driftwood varies along the coast, and St. Michael does not have the quantity to be found in other localities such as Shaktoolik, where tree trunks pile up knee-high on the beach.

Repairs on the bucket serve to chronicle changes over the years: they range from an old piece of birch bark stapled and glued to one end of the bottom to two pieces of modern plastic wire put through holes in the sides to anchor the bottom. The plug in the knothole was probably inserted shortly after the bucket was made, but other cracks were mended with adhesive tape. The wooden bail is fastened to the bucket with white string. Besides having the usual groove round the top and the bottom sides, there is also a semicircular groove on the bottom of the bucket. The grooves may be only decorative, but a groove placed under the bucket where it would not ordinarily be seen suggests to me that they may have had a magical meaning.

Fig. 40. Anonymous, Teller area. Trinket box. Birch bark, ivory strips. Late nineteenth century. Circumference 9″

Bentwood Trinket Box (figure 40)

There are few gifts that I have valued more than this well-made birch-bark trinket box, given to me in 1950 by Emma Willoya of Nome. Emma (she was always fondly known as Emma), told me that the box was from the Teller area and that she had had it for a long time. The small oval box is constructed like the bentwood bucket from St. Michael (fig. 39). The birch bark, which has been oiled, is lined with a stiff, heavy hide that is kept in place by friction. Small nails secure the overlapped ends of the birch bark, and two parallel ivory strips are inset, or sewn, with narrow pieces of skin outside the overlapped ends. The wooden lid fits tightly and is lifted off with a strip of rawhide.

Emma Willoya, a woman of dignity and of compassion for her own people, gave me the box quite unexpectedly when I left Nome at the end of summer 1950. I felt rather embarrassed to take it because I could think of only one thing I had done to prompt such a gift—I had given her some food left over from my summer's stay. I wish that Emma, who died in 1983, were alive to know that her thoughtfulness will be permanently remembered in this museum collection.

Some Thoughts about Dolls and Statues

Human Figurine of Wood (figure 41)

A small wooden doll was found on the beach of Nome during the gold rush of 1900 by the chief engineer of a ship. He gave it to the father of my next-door neighbor in Kenmore, Washington, who, in turn, gave it to me in 1962. This rather crudely made figure has no arms; its facial features are snipped out with gashes on a face set at about a twenty-degree angle to the neck; it has no sexual guideposts; and its feet are but nubbins at the end of bent legs—but it has a simplicity that packs a lot of power in a small space. It was not made to stand up, and since I wanted it upright on my desk (and after a fall had injured its feet), I mounted it on a block of wood dyed to match the original dark color of the doll (fig. 41).

It is uncertain whether this figure belonged to a child, or perhaps to a shaman. The Eskimo fathers made many dolls of ivory for children, and the mothers dressed them in furs, but from the scanty references to dolls or human figurines when the Eskimos were making them for their own use, it appears that wooden dolls were more often used by shamans, while ivory dolls were playthings for the girls. In the 1890s, however, Miner Bruce, a former reindeer superintendent turned collector, obtained two wooden dolls—a male and a female—that were dressed in typical fur finery from Port Clarence, but he did not explain whether these were children's dolls or figures made for sale. (VanStone 1976:45 and pl. 27b). People of the Port Clarence area had been making souvenirs for years. In 1867 *The Esquimaux,* a newspaper published at Port Clarence by the Western Union Telegraph contingent, reported that an Eskimo named Uta-

Fig. 41. Anonymous, Nome. Human figurine. Wood. Nineteenth century. Height 7⅜"

mana had explained that a long spell of bad weather in May was because the Natives were making miniature sleds and snowshoes, "of which we have recently bought so many. He seems to think that the manufacture of such articles at this time of year ridicules the elements, and makes them vent their spleen in consequence"—issue no. 9 (2 June 1867).

Unless information on the use and meaning was obtained at the time of collection, we can only conjecture about a specific doll or figurine, but we do know that carvings both of ivory and wood made in human shape were more than just "dolls." Large wooden figures have been used in various religious and secular ceremonies—by shamans for curing and magical acts, and as fertility figures for women. Three fertility figures, carved of wood by Numaiyuk of St. Lawrence Island, are in the University of Alaska Museum. According to Otto William Geist, who collected them during his archeological work on the island, they were given to sterile women in the hopes they would bear children. Geist, who visited Numaiyuk in 1927, said he was "a carver of the many dolls, idols, festishes, and ornamented household utensils fashioned from driftwood found in many of the island homes" (Geist and Rainey 1936:34. The three figurines are illustrated in Ray 1977: figs. 148–50).

E. W. Nelson also learned that dolls might bring about the preferred sex of a baby. "As a rule, married women are very anxious to have a son, and in case of long continued barrenness they consult a shaman, who commonly makes, or has the husband make, a small, doll-like image over which he performs certain secret rites, and the woman is directed to sleep with it under her pillow" (Nelson 1899:435).

Wooden dolls or statues were used indoors as centerpieces in numerous festivities as well as for memorials outdoors. Lavrentii A. Zagoskin, who explored southwest Alaska during 1842–1844, described an unusual "special ceremony," in which five nude wooden statues (two of them female), about 28 inches high, and "with arms bound in a special way and the legs only indicated by a line," each wearing a mask, were placed on the first bench of the ceremonial house. Each statue had a lamp burning in front of it, and later, after dancing, food was put before each one. According to the narrator of this information (Zagoskin wrote this at second hand, which is why it is so difficult to follow), these statues represented absent people from another village, who were being "married" in a mock ceremony. Apparently this was a kind of "asking festival," because as people placed the food before the statues, they said: "This is for you from our supplies; help us to more in the future." On the next day, the statues were put away in "their old place behind the kazhim and covered . . . over with birch bark and wood. The old men say that even their fathers do not remember when the statues were made" (Zagoskin 1967:229).

The most public display of large wooden figures was in Yup'ik territory, especially in the Kuskokwim River area, where memorial figurines in various shapes and sizes were erected in cemeteries. In the Smithsonian, I saw several of the memorial posts that Aleš Hrdlička, the Czechoslovakian archeologist, had brought back from the Kuskokwim in 1928, and had illustrated in his *Alaska Diary*. At the abandoned village of Akiachak, he photographed the cemetery with the figures fallen down. He wrote: "Figures with hands here, one of twin children. Five secured and sawed off, for packing. . . . All had eyes and mouth inlays of ivory" (Hrdlička 1944:311–12.) One of the figures, inlays missing, is shown in illustration 10. Distasteful as this apparent thievery may now seem to the descendants of the people represented in the cemetery, these unusual statues were saved for future generations because they had already been abandoned and left to decay.

I became especially interested in this aspect of Eskimo art because again it served as an example of differences between the Yup'ik and Inupiaq people. The Inupiat, who lived north of Norton Sound, did not commemorate the dead with sculpture or artistic monuments, although, like the Yupiit, they placed the dead person's possessions nearby for use in an afterlife. Some of the Yupi'k cemeteries did not contain the dead but were designed as memorial parks, a unique idea. Early accounts and photographs suggest that the monuments must have been spectacular, especially when placed in groups. Even in the 1930s, when all were falling down from neglect, and with their religious significance supplanted by new beliefs, vestiges of their former splendor still remained.[4]

Illus. 10. Memorial pole from Akiachak, Kuskokwim River, collected from the cemetery by Aleš Hrdlička, 1928. Height: 18¾". Ivory eyes and mouth inlays are missing. Courtesy of Smithsonian Institution, cat. no. 351,078

The Messenger Feast of 1912

Mask (figure 42)

In 1946, I was given a mask from Unalakleet which I later learned was very rare, because few masks have been saved from this area. This mask (fig. 42) has a most unusual configuration, made as if to represent a huge mouth. No one has been able to explain it to me, but its abstract form must surely have come from a shaman's dream. The mask is painted gray, with several applications of paint. The inside of the mouth, a large round hole on the left forehead, and a teardrop eye below it, are painted red. The right eye is unpainted. The large hole may be an eye, or a place to insert a carving or an appendage. Feathers were probably inserted above the lip, because stubs of quills are still stuck into the wood.

In the 1960s two people, Margaret Johnsson and Shafter Toshavik, who had participated in the last Inviting-In Feast (Messenger Feast) between St. Michael and Unalakleet in 1912, suggested to me that this mask might have been used at that time. However, Ernest W. Hawkes, a St. Michael schoolteacher who described this festival in a monograph, apparently accounted for all of the masks of the festival. He wrote: "At the conclusion of the feast I asked the old man for the masks which had been used in the dances. They are usually burned by the shaman after the ceremonies are over. I was much surprised the next day when the old fellow appeared with the masks and the whole paraphernalia of the dancers. . . . I believe he got around the religious difficulty by supplying an equal amount of wood for the sacrificial fire" (Hawkes 1913:4).

Yet Hawkes may not have obtained all of the masks. His reporting of the festival has so many omissions and varies so from the information that Mrs. Johnsson and Mr. Toshavik gave me that it seems a different ceremony. For example, Hawkes mentions only one chief at St. Michael and does not mention the two important headmen for the festival from each village; nor does he describe the months of preparation of songs and dances by each village, nor the many athletic contests held every day during the festival.

The Messenger Feast was celebrated all along the western Alaska coast by two villages, one inviting the other when food was abundant and the days were darkest, usually in January. In all accounts of the Messenger Feast (and even in its legendary origin) there are two headmen from each village, and messengers to send and receive the invitation. Mrs. Johnsson, who was fifteen when she attended from Unalakleet, and Mr. Toshavik, who was thirty at the time and a messenger, told me independently that the two headmen from Unalakleet were Katchatag (Mrs. Johnsson's uncle) and Tomron (pronounced Tungan by Toshavik); and from St. Michael, Anaurak (Andrew Anaurak) and Anakasak (Soxie).

Hawkes also writes that the "feast nearly came to grief owing to the over-zealous action of the young missionary in nominal charge of the Unalaklit," who had "appealed to the military commander

Fig. 42. Anonymous, Unalakleet. Mask. Wood, paint, quill stubs. About 1912. Height 9½"

of the district to put a stop to the whole thing." Hawkes, however, states that he intervened and persuaded the military commander, "a very liberal man," to let the festivities go on as planned (1913:2). Although unknown to Mrs. Johnsson, this may nonetheless have happened, but she remembered (in the village where the missionary was supposedly putting his foot down) the "months" of practicing dances and songs, as well as practicing them each night when they stopped with their dog teams in small villages en route to St. Michael.

When the Unalakleet people arrived in St. Michael, she and her brother Maurice Johnson (Johnson was her maiden name) accompanied her uncle and the other headman through the tunnel of the *kazigi* (ceremonial house), and up and through the floor opening. Hawkes does not describe this initial welcome in which, according to Mrs. Johnsson, each Unalakleet headman was led to his St. Michael counterpart (Katchatag to Soxie, and Tomron to Anaurak), "challenging" the latter to provide food and entertainment. Immediately after the challenge, the St. Michael women treated them to "all kinds of food"—boiled fish and meat, berries, and wild roots. After they had eaten, they were taken to the house where they would stay for the duration of the festivities, three or four days.

Hawkes's account of this event leaves the impression that it consisted only of dances and songs in the evening ceremonies. Besides his other omissions, he does not describe the many athletic games that filled the daytime hours, indoors and outdoors, as the young men vied for prizes in foot racing, dog team racing, and individual competitions of strength and agility. Although the Messenger Feast was always held between two friendly villages, a mock hostility was incorporated in all of the festivities along the coast—a "challenge" in the Unalakleet–St. Michael welcome; in others, a "welcoming" with men shooting arrows into the air, as in the Kauwerak Messenger Feast (Kakaruk and Oquilluk 1964:22). These acts reminded participants of past hostilities and former enemies, but with a peace reaffirmed in the winter festivities.

Animal Figurines

John Kanalook: Wooden Owl (figure 43)

This owl, made of birch wood, was possibly patterned after a nineteenth-century figurine used in ceremonies to obtain better hunting, in the Buckland area on the northeast coast of Seward Peninsula. Several wooden figurines, made in Buckland in 1951 by carver John Kanalook (Kaunaaluk), were brought by Charles Lucier, a biologist, to the University of Alaska Fairbanks, where he sold them to three lucky buyers: James W. VanStone, the University of Alaska Museum, and me. The museum purchased at least six figurines, which range in length from 4¼ inches (a duck) to 7 inches (a wolf). The other figures are a beluga whale, a bearded seal, a wolverine, and a caribou with its legs and antlers glued on. Each figurine has two tiny holes

Fig. 43. John Kanalook, Buckland. Owl sculpture. Wood with ivory eyes. 1952. 6" from beak to tip of tail

drilled on the back. A loop of baleen tied to a short length of braided sinew is still attached to each piece except the weasel, which has sinew passing through a hole to the under side and tied since it is so small, only 1¾ inches long (information from Dinah Larsen, 19 January 1994).

I illustrated the owl in *Eskimo Art* (1977: fig. 162), but I did not have detailed information at that time. Subsequently, VanStone sent me information that Lucier had copied from his notes, and while I was writing this section about the owl, Lucier sent me background details of his fieldwork and about Sannu Andrew Sunno, a Kangigmiut (Buckland) man, who had described for him the meaning of the carvings made by John Kanalook.

The birch wood carvings that Lucier sold to VanStone and me were not ordered and approved by Sannu, as were those in an earlier group, also made by Kanalook (these were the ones purchased by the museum), but they were made in the same manner as the originals, and Sannu had personally explained their use, which he knew at first hand, since he had witnessed Buckland hunting ceremonies in the early 1860s. Sannu was in his nineties when he talked to Lucier, who estimated his birthdate as 1857–59 because Sannu had remembered witnessing a total solar eclipse (1869) while living in Unalakleet when he was "this high" (shoulder high, about ten years old). He spoke to Lucier in both English and Inupiaq, the latter translated by Jessie Ralph (Tiasrik), who was born in 1898 in Selawik. The carver Kanalook was born about 1882 and possibly had witnessed similar hunting ceremonies as a child.

Lucier observed Kanalook's carving in a reindeer herder's apartment at Singiq (Elephant Point). Kanalook worked sitting cross-legged on his winter-caribou mattress, in a narrow, waist-high boxed-in bunk against a wall. His tools for his carving were an adze; a steel-bladed antler-shafted crooked knife; files; and, for final smoothing of an object, sandpaper (Lucier to author, 5 October 1994).

Information about these objects and their place in hunting ceremonies is now irretrievable. Although this owl can be enjoyed as a very fine piece of art, it becomes a living part of a forgotten ceremonial as we learn about the unusual circumstance of its carving; its place in a ceremony; and above all, the influence of a shaman in both the abstract esthetic sense (the carvings) and in the grim realities of the subsistence quest. (The following description is taken from Charles Lucier's notes of 1951, sent to me on 5 October 1994. Sannu's verbatim comments are in quotation marks.)

Hunting, both land and sea animals, and fishing were the mainstays of Eskimo life. When a Buckland man needed better luck in his hunting, he consulted a shaman, who usually "told the hunter to carve wooden figures of the food animals, birds, or fish that he wanted to catch," but no fur animals except wolves. (Lucier, however, stated that it was possible that a man could carve other non-food animals or birds if he needed such for a special use, for example, as an amulet.) "The hunter made the figures carefully . . . as realistically as he was able, making them about six inches or so long and showing as many characteristic features of the species as possible. For instance, a seal figure showed the eyes that were either inlaid with baleen (*suqaq*) or oily soot, the limbs, flippers and body openings: nostrils, mouth, ears, genital orifice and anus. He didn't indicate the backbones, ribs or other skeletal parts.

"The man made knife cuts in a certain place on each of the figures that he carved. When he had marked a carving with knife cuts, it was certain that the hunter would kill an animal of that species, and it would have marks identical to those knife marks on its body, in exactly the same places."

Each carving was made with a slot on the back for suspension from a horizontal pole placed at the back of the *qalgi* (ceremonial men's house, Buckland dialect) where the carvers and their families (including women) assembled in the spring when ice was still on the river. After the hunters had hung all of their carvings, "the shaman and the participating hunters gathered there [where the carvings were hanging]. The shaman began by drumming and singing. He didn't wear any sort of mask. While the shaman drummed and sang in the *qalgi*, some kind of power made the carved figures become alive," at which time no one present could eat or drink lest the power should harm him or her.

The shaman then asked each hunter, in turn, to sit on the floor in front of his own carvings, to "take a perfect, miniature arrow that was eight or nine inches long in one hand [and to] point the arrow's head toward a particular figure. The shaman would say to the hunter, 'Do you really recognize it? Do you find your mark? Do you kill it?'" If the hunter sincerely tried to follow the shaman's instructions, the carved animal would bleed where he had aimed his arrow. "The shaman repeated this procedure with each man until they had aimed at every figure that was hanging from the pole."

Next, "the shaman took the men [and their carvings of land animals or birds] to a secret place in the country, where they built a fire, and the shaman had each man throw his carvings into the fire." However, carvings of creatures that belonged in the water were taken by the hunters (in a group so that all of the men could be witnesses) to the river where there was a hole in the ice. The shaman instructed each man to put his carvings, one by one, into the water. "If a carving sank, it meant that the hunter would have good luck hunting that particular kind of animal; if the carving floated and wouldn't sink, it meant that the hunter who had made it would die soon, before he could hunt the animal. (This seems to be a rather dire prediction, since wood usually floats! Lucier, however, has explained that the swift Buckland River current would quickly sweep away the wooden figures, so perhaps the final disposition of the objects was not readily apparent.)

Ceremonies performed for prognostication were widespread throughout western Alaska, as was the use of oracles. One of the best-known oracles was a wooden doll, used in the so-called doll festival, celebrated not only by Eskimos from lower Yukon villages but also by the Athabascan people at Anvik in the interior, who had borrowed the practice from the Eskimos. Like the Buckland animals, this doll was also taken into the *kazigi,* where it became the center of various ceremonies. It was then wrapped in birch bark and hung in a tree in a secret place, where the shamans pretended "to consult [it] to ascertain what success will attend the season's hunting or fishing. If the year is to be a good one for deer [caribou] hunting, the shamans pretend to find a deer hair within the wrappings of the image"; and to foretell success in fishing, they would find a fish scale (Nelson 1899:494).

At the old village of Kauwerak in the Teller area on Seward Peninsula, a wooden face carved into the top of a post was placed in a corral to predict success in caribou hunting. The face, which was carved by a shaman, had eyes with red pupils, a big, open mouth with sharp teeth made of caribou leg bone, eyebrows and hair made from long caribou neck fur, but no ears. The shaman visited the face each morning for a prediction: caribou hunting would be poor that day if only a small amount of blood flowed from the mouth, but the hunters would get many caribou if blood ran heavily down both sides. No one knew how the blood appeared, but the man who told me about this said that the shaman had probably mixed crushed alder bark or ocher with water or urine.

I do not have information about the place of owls in Buckland culture, but in reviewing the literature about Eskimo subsistence throughout western Alaska, including ethnographies and travelers' observations, I find that the owl is scarcely ever mentioned. Reports of a village's natural larder invariably mention fowl in variations of the phrase: "The hunters take innumerable geese, ducks, ptarmigan, swans, and even sandhill cranes," but rarely an owl. Owls, however, were not entirely neglected by the Eskimos, and their omission in accounts probably resulted from lack of observation by the authors, since owls are generally nocturnal and do not congregate in huge flocks, as do ducks and geese.

The owl—or the spirit of the owl—has been made as masks. I know of two of them: one collected about 1890 from St. Michael by H. M. W. Edmonds, and now in the Hearst Museum of Anthropology (formerly the Lowie Museum) at the University of California at Berkeley; and one collected about 1880 from the lower Yukon River by E. W. Nelson (Nelson 1899:pl. xcv; Ray and Blaker 1967:pl. 16). These masks apparently were used in festivals to propitiate the spirits of animals for better hunting, but there is no information as to whether the masks represented a tutelary or were among the many figures used in conjunction with songs and dances performed to persuade the game animals to give them a good harvest next year.

Owls were occasionally eaten, although with the abundance of other fowl, hunting them would have been wasteful effort except in time of famine. At Wales, the early schoolteacher Harrison Thornton wrote that the "snowy owl," which measured twenty-four inches long with a five foot wingspread and weighed five pounds, was "delicious to eat" (Thornton 1931:205). Owl feathers were also used. At St. Michael, Edmonds said that the people there considered the "perfectly white skin [the feathers of the 'white owl'] to be very valuable" (Ray, ed., 1966:43). Many Yup'ik masks were decorated around the rim with halos of caribou fur and bird feathers, including those of the owl. Nelson collected and illustrated a large mask of "some species of waterfowl" and two small masks (that he called "maskettes"), all of which were decorated with the feathers of the horned owl. He did not know how the two maskettes were used, but thought that the large mask "was used in festivals connected with obtaining success in the hunt," because wooden flaps on either side had various game animals drawn on them (Nelson 1899:404, 410–11, pls. xcix, no. 1, and ciii, nos. 2 and 6). Although he called that mask a "species of waterfowl," its configuration suggests that it could well be an owl.[5]

Peter J. Seeganna: Wooden Walrus (figure 44)

This wooden walrus, which I think is one of the best sculptures made by an Inupiaq man of this century, has bittersweet memories, foremost of which is the untimely death of artist Peter J. Seeganna in 1974 of a heart attack. He was born on 30 July 1938, in Nome, of King Island parents, and despite his youthful acceptance of much of western culture, he was definitely Inupiaq in outlook. This combination in both his art and his personal life made him an inventive and inquiring human being (see illus. 5, page 46).

By the time I met Peter in 1968, he was an accomplished artist and had been employed as an arts and crafts assistant for the U.S. Indian Arts and Crafts Board in Sitka, Alaska, where he won several art awards between 1964 and 1968. When the Sitka workshop terminated, he returned to Nome and agreed to organize and supervise a

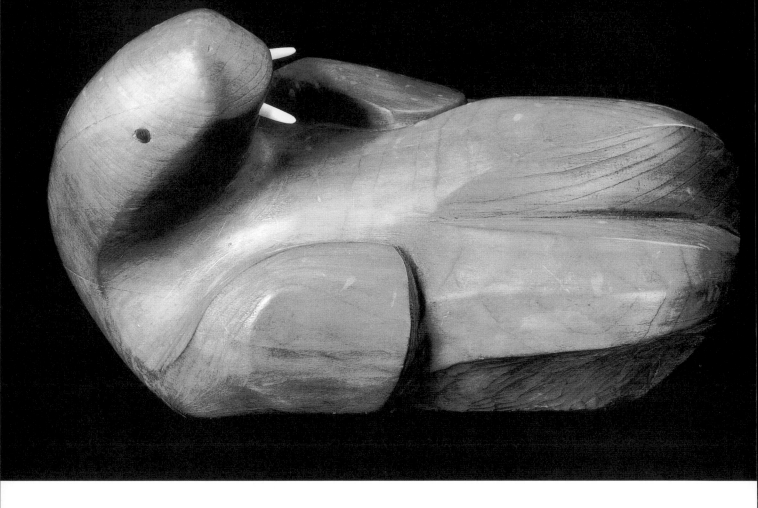

new cooperative for Inupiaq artists: Sunarit Arts and Crafts Associates. The cooperative had not been operating long that summer of 1968, but even then I could sense Peter's disappointment that there was not more enthusiasm among the young carvers to participate in the association, and especially to explore innovative ideas. Peter had grown up in the old carving tradition, but he also had a vision of redefining Eskimo art. This he did with his sculpture in both wood and stone, and in his woodblock prints.

Sunarit Associates had a separate building at that time, but members of Sunarit also sold their work in King Island Village, located on the beach west of Nome. The village at that time (as in 1955) was still an active aggregate of summer dwellers from the island with a few permanent inhabitants. The expanse of tundra and sandy ground was a playground for children the clock around during the summer days of almost twenty-four-hours' light, and, as thirteen years before, the tour buses still deposited tourists at the community

Fig. 44. A and B.
Peter J. Seeganna, King Island.
Walrus sculpture. Wood with
baleen eyes, ivory tusks. 1968.
Length 8¼"

house to watch the nightly dances and to purchase souvenirs from the display table.

I tried to attend as many of the dances as possible. On the souvenir table one evening I noticed this carved walrus (fig. 44), looking huge and wonderfully out of place (though only 8¼ inches long) among the usual small carvings and fur products. Putting this unusual piece of art on the table for consideration by typical tourists was part of a marketing experiment Peter was conducting to explore sales of non-traditional Eskimo art in a souvenir-buying setting. He wanted to know how quickly it might sell, and who the buyer would be. He had set a price of fifty dollars, which was not high for the piece in 1968, but was substantially higher than the little ivories at five or six dollars. It had other characteristics that an average tourist would probably take into consideration before buying: it did not look "Eskimo"; it was made of wood, not ivory (the material most closely associated with Eskimo products); it was larger than the ivories; and finally, it was made in an untraditional style—at least, not in the style illustrated in the tourist brochures—although it was a recognizable walrus with its two ivory tusks and its inlaid eyes of baleen. I wanted to buy it as soon as I saw it, but I gave in to Peter's experiment, which had begun that evening with the first group of tourists.

I left for the village of Wales the next day, regretful of a lost opportunity and convinced that I would never see the walrus again, as I fully expected it to be winging its way out of the Nome airport in a day or two in someone's carry-on bag. So it was with amazement and both sadness and joy that I returned ten days later and saw that it was still on the table—sadness that one of the approximately 600 tourists who had been to the dances had not had the esthetic sense to have bought it, and joy that it was now *mine*— and at its reduced price of forty dollars! For a long time afterwards I thought: so much for the Nome tourist and art appreciation!

As mentioned earlier, most of the houses in King Island Village were swept away in a storm of 1973, and the islanders, who had left the island permanently in 1966, moved into Nome and other places. Small ivory carvings are still sold in gift shops, but sculpture like Peter Seeganna's walrus has now come into its own as a part of the wider sphere of art, and artists of Peter's generation and younger now exhibit their work in galleries where they command respect and prices equal to any in the world.

I have had the walrus on display in our house where every visitor can see it. Invariably—and to my surprise and delight—every person not only wants to look at it but to hold it. Consequently, the wood has developed a slight patina throughout the years as many hands have touched the past and the vision of an exceptional young artist.

Pictorial Engraving
or Eskimo Scrimshaw

As long as two thousand years ago, the people of St. Lawrence Island, who were closely related to the Siberians, used metal points to incise geometric and linear designs on their ivory dolls, harpoon heads, throwing-stick counterbalances, and many unidentified objects. For more than 1,500 years these people of succeeding cultures, called Okvik, Old Bering Sea, and Punuk, wrought some of the most unusual ornamental art in Eskimo history. With the exception of the Ipiutak period (A.D. 1000) at Point Hope, this kind of art was not present on the mainland of western Alaska. But by about A.D. 1500, everywhere, ornamentation of objects became simpler or even nonexistent. However, a new development in graphic art—the portrayal of realistic scenes on ivory and bone—was emerging, possibly as early as the eighteenth century in Thule culture. By the time the first foreign explorers arrived in Alaska during the early nineteenth century, it was a full-blown art.

How and when this unique art began is shrouded in mystery. The archeological record tells us little because most of the so-called prehistoric sticklike drawings on bone combs were purchased in Point Hope and Wales, and the few that have been recovered by archeologists appear to be late Thule, if that. The question is whether pictorial engraving was an original Eskimo idea or was borrowed from the Russian traders in Siberia. Russians were in eastern Siberia as early as the seventeenth century, and Russian goods were crossing the Bering Strait to Native Alaskan markets before the first explorers came to these shores. Knowing the general area of origin and the

Inupiaq propensity to copy, we can assume that the idea probably was borrowed from the Russians.

Drill Bows and Snow Beaters

Bow drill handles (called drill bows) with pictorial scenes were the first objects with this kind of engraving to be collected by the early European explorers to the Bering Strait area, which was the center of pictorial work: James Cook in his expedition of 1778, Otto von Kotzebue in 1816, and Frederick William Beechey in 1826–27. All visitors thereafter collected a few, but the largest collection by far was made by Edward William Nelson on his winter trip to Seward Peninsula in 1879 (Ray 1977: 25–27; see Ray 1982b for a detailed discussion of pictorial engraving).

Other objects were engraved with graphic scenes, but the drill bow appears to have been the overwhelming favorite, despite the extremely small surface that all drill bows provided—a half-inch at the most. Drill bows were four-sided, triangular, or two-sided with convex surfaces. I have been unable to learn of any religious or cere-monial use for the engravings, which appear to be diaries in ivory, and, depending on the artist and the village, range in subject matter from group pursuits like whaling and walrus hunting, dancing, and intervillage visits, to individual activities such as hanging up meat, tending a cooking fire, or performing the still-popular "Eskimo high kick." But if these were diaries as well as useful tools (a bow drill was used mainly to bore holes), why were they parted with so easily? When Nelson visited Cape Nome and Sledge Island in 1879, the combined adult male population numbered probably no more than thirty five, but he obtained twenty three drill bows, and some of these were unfinished. (About 55 percent of all drill bows collected by Nelson were unfinished.)

All of the scenes undoubtedly depict personal experiences, but we can only guess what they signify, because collectors rarely obtained a meaning. W. J. Hoffman, who discussed and illustrated part of Nelson's collection in *The Graphic Art of the Eskimos,* hired a Kodiak Eskimo–Russian man, Vladimir Naomoff, to interpret the pictures and symbols. But anything that Naomoff told Hoffman was spuri-ous, because the Kodiak people did not engrave drill bows, and they lived in a culture somewhat foreign to the Bering Strait Eskimos. Naomoff's trying to "explain" the symbols was something like a Hopi man trying to explain the meaning of a Tlingit totem pole.

I have always used the term "engraving" because I have considered "scrimshaw" to be the artistic prerogative of the Yankee sailor. However, the term "Eskimo scrimshaw" or simply "scrimshaw" for Inupiaq engraving is now used more frequently than when I began my research more than forty years ago, and I suppose that it does impart more specificity to an art form than does "engraved ivory," especially for the uninitiated. Nonetheless, in this book I shall continue to use the words "engravings" and "engraved ivory" for this art form, but "scrimshaw" does have a nice ring to it!

Ivory Wand or Snow Beater (figure 45)

The two oldest pieces in the collection are an ivory wand or snow beater (fig. 45), and a drill bow (fig. 46), both of which I purchased through Sotheby's auction sales. Both date from the nineteenth century, the former having a documented date in the 1860s. The wand was originally offered for sale by Sotheby's in October 1983 (Sale 5096), in a group of artifacts collected by George W. Klinefelter, who, according to the catalog, was "probably assigned to the work of connecting the two continents by telegraph, via the Amoor River, and Bering Straits [sic]." Indeed he was. He was second in command of the forty-man contingent of workers at Port Clarence (between present-day Brevig Mission and Teller), where a four-building settlement called Libbysville (after Daniel Libby, the commander) was established on 17 September 1866. This was one of four principal sections of line-building that the Western Union Telegraph Company inaugurated in 1864 (the others were in British Columbia, Siberia, and Norton Sound, Alaska), but the company ceased work when the Atlantic Cable was a success in 1867.

This engraved wand was again offered for sale in 1986 (Sale 5465), now termed a "presentation knife," although the first sale had described it as "a long curving snowknife or shoehorn engraved on both sides with numerous animals and scenes of daily life, the pierced handle bound with hide." This is the only engraved piece of this shape that I have seen, and it is possible that it had another use before it was engraved to be sold, since it is shaped like snow beaters from this area

The technique, design elements, and permanence of color in the bold incisions are excellent. Although the piece was supposedly collected at Libbysville, the artist and his home village are unknown. Libbysville, in its short life, became a magnet for Eskimos, and a "hotel" was built for those who came from coastal villages or from

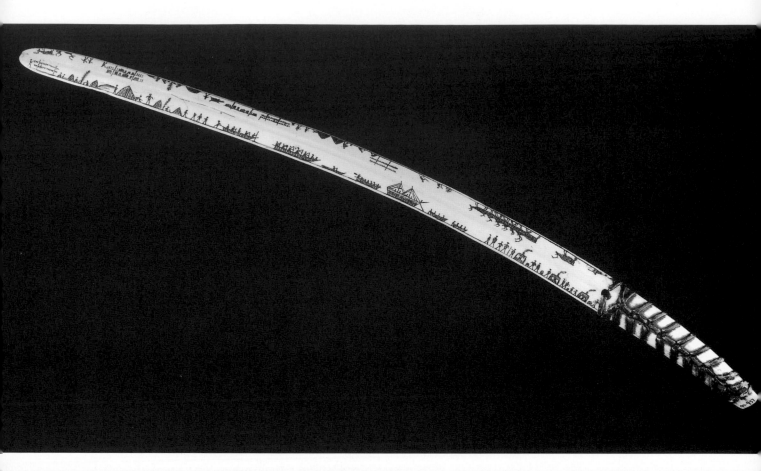

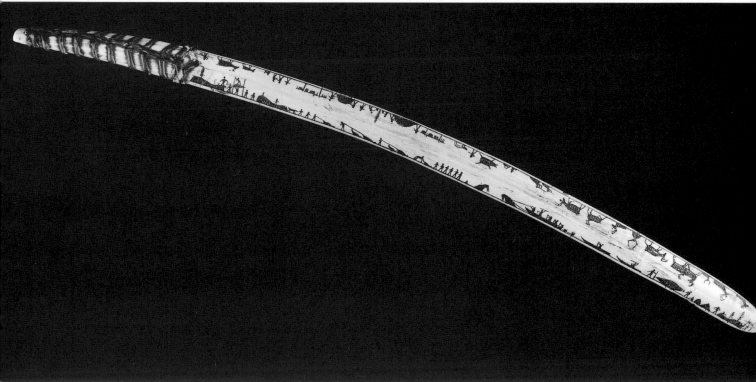

Fig. 45. Anonymous, Port
Clarence or Kauwerak. Snow
beater. A and B: reverse sides
shown. Walrus ivory engraved
with activity scenes of Eskimo
and white men. Collected by
George W. Klinefelter in 1866.
Length 18⅝"

Kauwerak, located inland about thirty miles away. A Kauwerak man probably engraved this piece, because people from this village were constant visitors. A ship was even named for their chief, Kamokin.

The subject matter reflects the lifestyle of Seward Peninsula Eskimos during the summer. The scenes of this two-sided piece are engraved on four baselines, one on each edge. Libbysville activities are placed on half of one of the baselines: men, buildings, and a ship and tenders. The foreigners are drawn with a slash on the head representing a hat. The Libbysville buildings are also found on drill bows collected from Kauwerak by Johan Adrian Jacobsen, a Norwegian collector, in 1882 (Der Königlichen Museen zu Berlin, 1884, pl. 9, no. 16, and pl. 10, no. 7).[1]

The other half of the Libbysville baseline depicts typical Eskimo pursuits and scenes: conical tents, a rack with fish, campfires with smoke represented as a feather, people, and umiaks and a kayak going out to the ship. On the opposite baseline (fig. 45A) is a caribou hunting scene with three men carrying rifles, and two fishing camps, one with two double-row fish-drying racks and the other with a rounded tent, a campfire, and two meat-drying racks.

On the reverse side (fig. 45B), one baseline has the following scenes: winter homes, people, a dog, elevated caches, conical tents, three men pulling seals home, and men in an umiak and two kayaks hunting walrus. On the other baseline two men are shooting at ten caribou near a fishing camp with rounded tents and the ubiquitous campfire and fish racks.

Although this piece was probably engraved by a man living in an inland village, he undoubtedly hunted seals and walrus on the coast with a partner from a coastal village, or was permitted to hunt in a coastal area. Villages in the Bering Strait area had formed alliances with other villages—especially between the mainland and the islands—to share resources. The Kauwerak people went regularly to Port Clarence to hunt seals and *ugruk* (bearded seals), and they were known to hunt walrus with King Islanders. A walrus hunting scene on a Kauwerak bow was not unusual, for Jacobsen collected one from the village itself in 1882 (ibid:pl. 10, no. 13).

Drill Bow (figure 46)

This drill bow is filled with a dizzying array of activities. Stick-figure people (twenty-three on each of the two broad sides of this four-sided bow) are dynamos in their various activities—legs apart, arms upraised, running, smoking pipes, shooting a gun, tending a fish

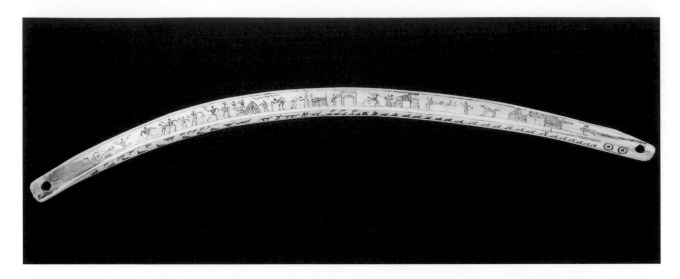

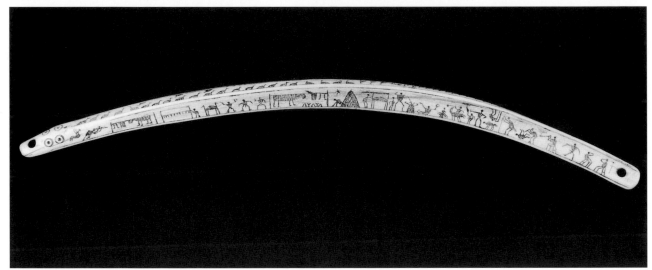

rack, jumping, wrestling, throwing; even the four bent figures walking with a staff seem full of pep. Each side of the bow has a conical tent and a fish rack, but no outdoor fire with its attendant person. One side (fig. 46A) shows two square buildings, apparently a white man's dwellings, and, on the same side, almost invisible in a crowd of fourteen Eskimos, is a man with a broad-brim hat, arms akimbo, smoking a pipe—a foreigner (standing still!), the only passive figure on the entire drill bow. The hat style (a slash atop his head) and the arms akimbo were both identifying devices in the early engravings to represent the non-Native person. No provenience or date accompanied this bow, but it probably came from the Norton Sound area because of a similar engraving style on several objects that E. W. Nelson collected there in 1879.

Fig. 46. Anonymous, probably Norton Sound. Drill bow. A and B: reverse sides shown. Walrus ivory with engravings. Nineteenth century. Length 13″

The two narrow sides, each a quarter-inch at the widest, tapering to half that size at the ends, are covered with rows of seals, most of which are incised and filled with black color. However, fourteen seals on one side and nineteen on the other are left uncolored. In the midst of a row of seals are two walrus heads facing each other, and in another scene on the same side (fig. 46B), which seems out of place, two men, one with a drawn bow, are near four unidentifiable creatures that look like ostriches. Two circle-dots are drilled at the end of three sides of the bow.

Cribbage Boards and Walrus Tusks

The demise of drill bow art and the development of large-scale graphics on cribbage boards and big walrus tusks coincided with the establishment of American trading companies on the mainland of northwest Alaska after Russia sold Alaska to the United States in 1867. By the 1890s there was scarcely an engraved drill bow left in western Alaska, the collectors of the 1880s (and before) having cleaned out the supply. During the 1890s, Miner W. Bruce, a reindeer man turned trader and collector, who knew the Bering Strait area well, was able to obtain only three engraved objects (of a total of 866 artifacts) at Kotzebue Sound, and only six engraved objects, five of them souvenir pipes (of 425 artifacts), from Port Clarence (VanStone 1976: 1980).

The drill bow artists transferred their talents to the making of souvenir objects, like the pipes and whole tusks, and though these Eskimo scenes showed a record of their activities, they were not made for the artist's own remembrance or for possible communication with his peers but were aimed at a world he would never know. The new walrus-tusk art began sometime in the 1870s when the Alaska Commercial Company at St. Michael began trading for walrus tusks, and either gave or sold the tusks to men for engraving, because there was no walrus hunting in that area. The Yup'ik of St. Michael did not engrave ivory, but St. Michael became the center for souvenir pipes and tusks when northerners immigrated there for trade and work. Guy Kakarook, whose artistry is described next, moved to St. Michael from the village of Atnuk on Golovnin Bay, more than sixty miles to the north.

Guy Kakarook: Tusk (figure 47)

While some of the artists transferred drill bow motifs into larger size on their larger material, they also engraved western illustrations, often on the same piece. This tusk engraved by Guy Kakarook is a good example of work done by an artist who was still steeped in the old tradition, but who, in later years, made a successful transition to a fully recognizable western style of representational art in another medium—that of painting and drawing on paper. Two notebooks, each with thirty-two scenes of Eskimo life (winter scenes, dated 1895; summer scenes, 1903), are now in the United States National Museum (Smithsonian Institution), where they attest to Kakarook's talents.

The engraving on the Kakarook tusk is fairly heavy. The black color, which is probably India ink, has weathered time well and is probably as black as when applied. Kakarook undoubtedly engraved this tusk during the time span of his notebooks, because it was originally purchased in 1904 during the St. Louis Universal Exposition by Dwight Brown, a St. Louis jeweler. Furthermore, Kakarook depicted the same people—a man and a woman dressed in Siberian garb—on the tusk and in a drawing in the summer book, shown here in illustration 11.

The tusk is rather oval in shape, with two broad sides and a narrow one on the inside curve. Kakarook engraved a wide spectrum of Eskimo life, a variety that rivals the drill bow subject matter. One side (fig. 47A) has two parallel sets of drawings, one above the other. The bottom has (from left to right) an Eskimo family of man, woman, and child; the two Siberians; two people wrestling, watched by two people; an Eskimo village consisting of three big houses, a *kazigi* (community house), raised storage caches, and an umiak on a rack. In the top section are (left to right) two walrus heads, two whales, a seal head, a unicorn (of all things), and Kakarook's signature, which is exactly like his in the notebooks. Kakarook no longer used the old feather symbol to represent smoke from a chimney, but instead drew a series of circles.

On the opposite broad side (fig. 47B), a sequence of animals is engraved in separate sections, including a wolverine, fox, polar bear, grizzly bear, two caribou with an eagle above ready to pounce, and three separate caribou. The narrow side has two opposing baselines incised with maritime activities, a kayak on a sled, a man with a spear hunting seals near mounds of ice, and two more kayaks in the water. On the other edge are five kayaks, with a man in each. The

Kakarook gui

Illus. 11. Guy Kakarook painted this Siberian man and woman in a notebook now in the Smithsonian Institution, cat. no. 316,702, notebook no. 2, neg. no. 1713D. He engraved the same figures on the tusk in figure 47

ends of the tusk are finished with longitudinal gashes and the spurred-line motif, a design element that dates back several hundred years.

Kakarook's notebooks were collected by Sheldon Jackson, Alaska's first agent of education, while he was a passenger on the revenue cutter *Bear* as he inspected the newly established schools in western Alaska between 1890 and 1902. Early in the course of my research at the National Museum, I saw one of the notebooks on display, open to a drawing, on the back wall of a case. This notebook was new to me, and I was eager to inspect it at first hand. But bureaucracy is a formidable foe, and entreaties to various levels of responsibility fell on deaf ears. Finally, a senator intervened on my behalf (no, it was not an Alaskan senator!), and in that magic moment I learned about the power of a senator. It was providential that the display case was

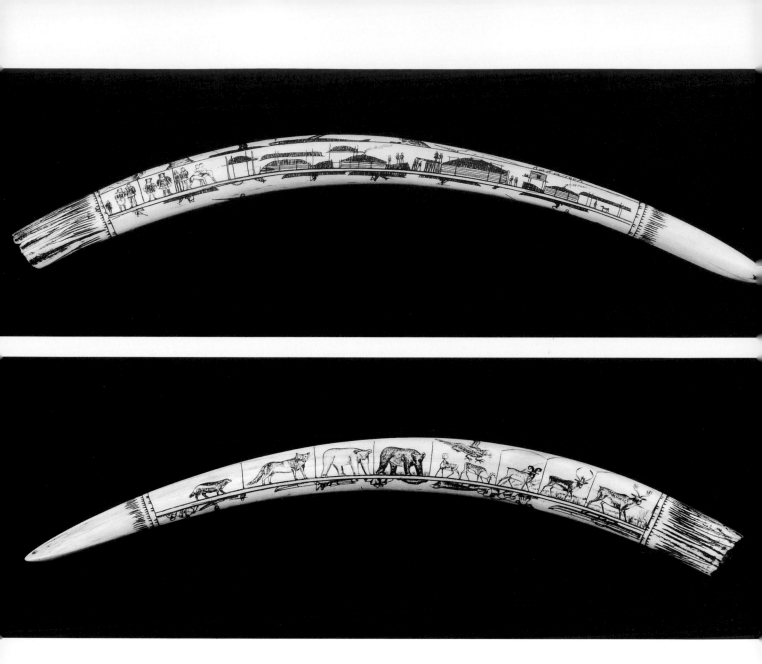

opened, because the notebook, we discovered, was saved thereby from certain ruin, its having been held to the wall with thumbtacks.

Jackson provided no notes about the drawings, so we do not know under what conditions they were made and subsequently purchased. Lack of data, except for date and place, apparently characterized most of Jackson's acquisitions, and may be partly explained by his obsessive collecting of everything he laid his eyes on. In the first fourteen years of the new museum he helped found in Sitka—the Sheldon Jackson Museum—he deposited more than 3,000 objects, whereas "many of today's museums would be duly proud to acquire more than 200 pieces for their permanent collections annu-

Fig. 47. Guy Kakarook, St. Michael. Walrus ivory tusk with engravings. A and B: reverse sides shown. About 1904. 22¾"

ally" (Hulbert 1987: xi). In addition, he kept many objects for his personal use, and the two Kakarook notebooks were included in a purchase of almost 800 items by the Smithsonian Institution from Sheldon Jackson's daughter in 1921. (See Ray 1971c for examples of Kakarook's watercolors.)

Kakarook's old friends told me in the 1960s that they did not know he was an artist (Kakarook died about 1906), but he and his stepson, Joe Austin, were well-known ivory artists in St. Michael in the 1890s. A number of Joe's works are in public and private collections, signed variously as Joe Kakasook, Joe Kakavook, Joe Skakayook, Joe Kakararzook, and Joe Kakgavgook. These works were done in 1901 or before, while he was still living in St. Michael and before the census taker had changed his name to Austin, which apparently was necessary in view of the many variations of his Eskimo name. It is a bit mysterious why Joe, who is said to have been an interpreter in Nome, thus variously spelled his Eskimo name, but he perhaps did not read or write, and so copied his name as provided by the person who bought his work.

The Kakarooks were the only St. Michael artists who signed their ivory work, to my knowledge, and only a few other names have come down to us. A tantalizing collection of artifacts made by a John Erikson of the State Bank of Seattle in the 1890s lists a few names: "Joe Kakavok" (Joe Austin); "Emeli" or "Emelik," who was an "Eskimo of Pitmiktalik Norton Sound"; "Auvoyak, Eskimo of Unalaklut [Unalakleet]"; and "Omealik . . . Big Diomede Island." The collection eventually went to the Baltimore Museum of Art, but it was sold before I became aware of its existence, and I have been unable to get descriptions or photographs of the pieces. Emelik apparently engraved scenes similar to those of the Kakarooks, for, according to the list, one of his tusks illustrated the "Village and Mission of Unalaklut," and another illustrated "the site of the Reindeer station on the Unalaklut river."

Tusk (figure 48)

Nome was founded at the mouth of the Snake River, on the site of a seasonal fishing camp, after gold was discovered on Anvil Creek in 1898. When the world learned about the gold strike, tens of thousands of would-be millionaires rushed to the new town, and the souvenir capital of western Alaska shifted from St. Michael to Nome. The gold rush also shifted Eskimo trading practices forever, as all traders—even the Siberians—turned to Nome instead of the accus-

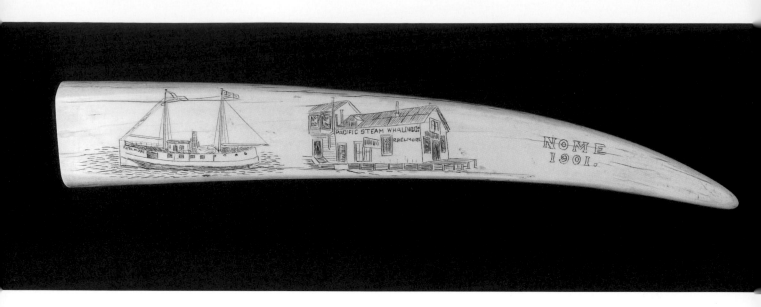

Fig. 48. Anonymous, Nome. Walrus ivory tusk with engravings. Probably the work of a non-Eskimo. 1901. 16"

tomed centers of Kotzebue, Point Spencer, and St. Michael. The newcomers formed a huge pool of customers who bought almost everything that was made by an Eskimo—implements, clothing, art work, and, equally acceptable, objects of ivory and wood made strictly as souvenirs. As in St. Michael, engravings of Eskimo nostalgia on ivory were among the most popular items. The souvenir trade of Nome started off with a bang and has continued as a healthy business ever since.

The subject matter of this tusk, a large ship and a large building, is unusual. Buildings were rarely engraved as single, large structures on cribbage boards and tusks but instead were components of a town or village, as in the panorama scenes of Nome (see fig. 49). This 16-inch piece exemplifies the quandary in which we sometimes find ourselves when trying to identify an object's origin. In this case, the date (1901), the place (Nome, Alaska), and the name (Pacific Steam Whaling Company) are probably not in question, but I suspect that the work was not done by an Eskimo engraver. Besides the unusual subject matter, the style and quality of the engraving are somewhat different from that of Eskimo scrimshaw. One of the mystifying aspects of this tusk is the name (R. P. Elmore) on both the ship and the building. I have been unable to find this name in accounts of early Nome, and John Bockstoce, the chronicler of commercial steam whaling history in the Arctic, does not know the name. But the Pacific Steam Whaling Company did have an office in Nome, and since this company "was in fact chartered to do freighting as well as mining . . . this station would have neatly suited their business strategy" (Bockstoce to author, 26 September 1993). Perhaps Elmore was an employee who wanted to be remembered in ivory.

More than one white man tried his hand at "Eskimo carving" during Nome's early days when walrus tusks were plentiful. One such object was an unusual cribbage board, reported (but not illustrated) in the 12 August 1903 issue of *The Nome Nugget*. It was made by a man named Hallie Heacock, who began engraving the tusk in Nome but finished it in Dawson, Yukon Territory. He used the same scenes that were favorites of Eskimo artists at that time: on one side, a hunter shooting at a polar bear, walrus heads rising out of the water, an Eskimo in his kayak, and a "deer"; on the reverse side, more Alaskan scenes, including an engraving of the steamer *Nome City*.

Cribbage Board (figure 49)

The most famous artist of Nome before the disastrous influenza epidemic of 1918 was Happy Jack, or Angokwazhuk (about whom more will be said), but other men also engraved cribbage boards and tusks with considerable skill. A rather ubiquitous subject is a panorama of the coast, from Snake River at the west end of Nome, to Cape Nome (a distance of about fourteen miles, measured from Snake River), but we do not know who engraved these panoramic scenes. The panorama always covers the entire side of a tusk, usually the reverse side of a cribbage board. The town of Nome, in this instance, has been copied from a photograph taken from the sea. It is not to scale, for though the town extends only two miles, it takes up half of the tusk. I have seen several of these panoramic engravings, always with a date incised in the ivory, the earliest dated 1903, and the latest, 1910.

This cribbage board of 1909 is big—28½ inches long and weighing 3½ pounds (fig. 49A). Cribbage holes are on the inside curve, so both ends were raised off the table, resting on three wooden pegs, when a game was in progress. On the left of the holes are two large walrus lying on a cake of ice, and between the holes are two seals, two birds, and a bee. An Eskimo village is engraved on the remaining length of the tusk (15 inches), but it is a two-tiered scene. On the upper half is an Eskimo village of four houses, four caches, an umiak on a rack, and fifty people, all standing. On the lower half are two tent settlements (thirty-five western-style tents in one, and forty-two in the other) with two groups of white men standing

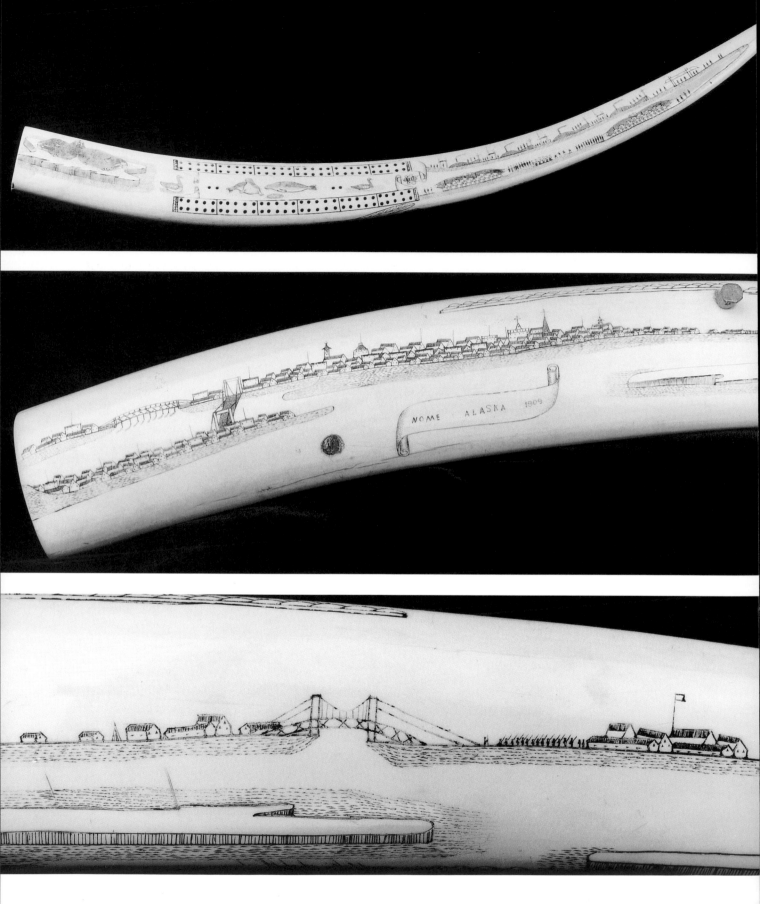

Pictorial Engraving or Eskimo Scrimshaw

Fig. 49. Anonymous, Nome. Cribbage board. A, B, and C: reverse sides and detail shown. Walrus ivory. Top side engraved with an Eskimo village and a contingent of soldiers; reverse engraved with panorama from Nome to Cape Nome. 1909. 28½"

between them, watching five drummers and four dancers on the lower half. A fascinating aspect of the people on this board is their seeming inertia, in contrast to the lively, busy people on the old drill bows. Except for the entertainers on this tusk, the people stand as if they were statues.

The coastal scene on the opposite side (fig. 49B) plainly shows the famous Geiger Bridge, built in 1900 by William Geiger, who made a tidy sum charging people to cross the Snake River. Ice cakes float in front of the town. The Nome River to the east is represented by a bridge, and a contingent of soldiers stand at attention at Fort Davis, a military installation established shortly after the gold rush (fig. 49C). This group of fourteen soldiers and a leader is one of the most amazing bits of engraving that I have seen. To the naked eye, the little group looks like a patch of grass or a tiny picket fence, because each soldier is only 0.04 inches high. But that's not all. Barely perceptible without a magnifying glass is a slight slash over each soldier's shoulder—his gun, slanting to the sky!

Cribbage Board (figure 50)

Another subject that was popular with early-day Nome ivory artists was an elongated map of the coastline, which usually extended from Cape Prince of Wales at Bering Strait southward to Unalakleet. These ivory maps were made by the dozens, and this collection has three different coastal designs. The earliest one, dated 8 September 1909, on the top face of the cribbage board (fig. 50A), has on its reverse side one of the most ambitious maps I've seen. It includes a huge "Eastern Siberia" (a feature not usually engraved on the maps) and extends from beyond Shishmaref, north of Cape Prince of Wales, to a mysterious big "Gulf" beyond the Yukon River (fig. 50B). The color is faint, and the animals are awkwardly drawn; but I like the map, the expressions on the animals' faces, and the nicely engraved eagle on the top, butt end. We cannot forget the date that this piece was made, because another "1909" is engraved under the eagle. There is a five-pointed star on each end of the cribbage holes, and between them are (left to right) a walrus, a bear with a fuzzy coat, and a seal. To the right of the holes are a sleeping (or dead?) walrus and a seal on an ice cake, and at the tip, a walking fox.

The two narrow sides also have engravings. On one (left to right), there are a ribbon seal, a fish, a caribou, a muskrat (?), and a branch with leaves; on the other (from tip end, left to right), two branches with leaves, a fish, and a beaver (?).

113

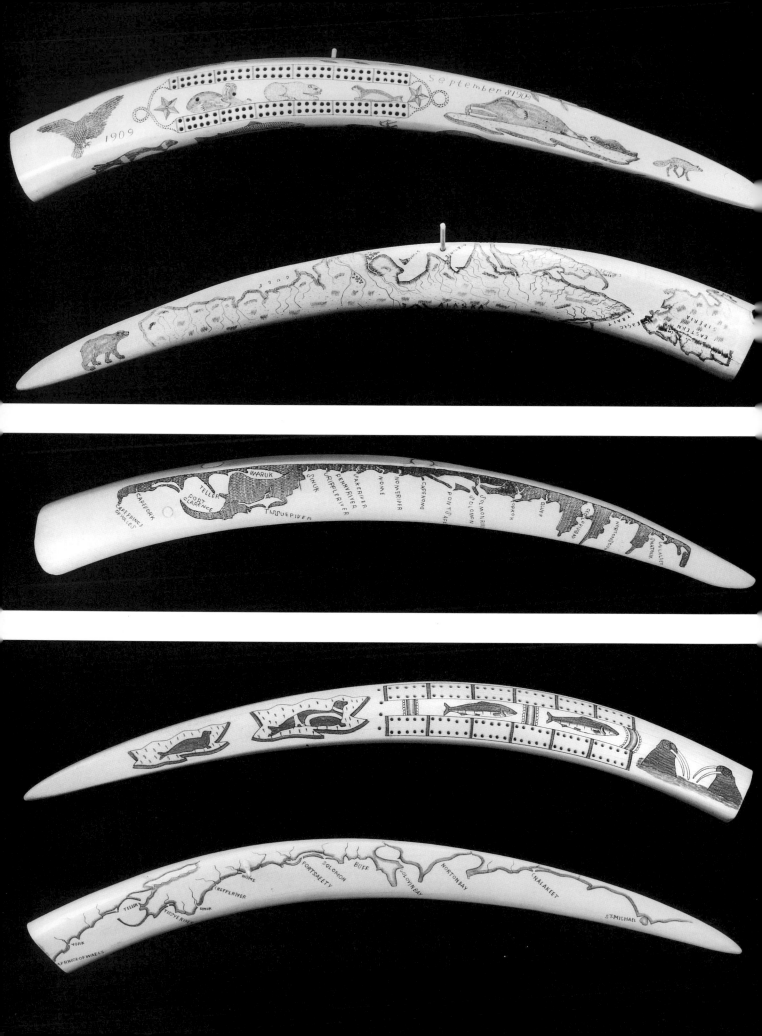

Fig. 50. Anonymous, Nome. Cribbage board. A and B: reverse sides shown. Walrus ivory. Reverse side shows map extending from "Eastern Siberia" to "Gulf." Dated September 8, 1909. 25½"

Fig. 51. Anonymous, probably Nome or King Island. Walrus ivory tusk with engraved map. About 1915. 20¼"

Fig. 52. Anonymous, Nome. Cribbage board. A and B: reverse sides shown. Walrus ivory tusk engraved with animals and a map. Early 1930s. 21"

Tusk (figure 51)

Another style of map, and the most common, is an attenuated coastline stretching from beyond Unalakleet to Cape Prince of Wales, on which the incisions are made by rocking a graver back and forth on the ivory. This small female tusk is engraved on only one side. The man who made this map apparently could not read, for he misspelled many names that he copied from a map: "Tissuepiver" (Tissue River), "Unlaleet" (Unalakleet), and Ckolovin-bav (Golovnin Bay), for example. This map was probably engraved by a King Island man, about 1915.

Cribbage Board (figure 52)

The third map in this collection, which is on the reverse side of a neatly engraved but rather unimaginative cribbage board of the early 1930s, has yet another interpretation of the coastline. The ivory is still quite white, and I think that it was made later than the other two, but the engraver also misspelled many names. This engraver was otherwise a precise worker, and his coastline is of exemplary neatness, although the two seals resting on an ice cake, the two fish, and the two walrus heads with extremely long tusks on the top side are trite and uninspired.

Happy Jack and His Ivory Art

Happy Jack had no equal during his lifetime in either engraving or sculpture. So far as we know, he did not engrave maps or panoramic views of Nome, or any other town, but instead used seascapes and mountain ranges as background for his many engravings of village and hunting scenes, and of animals, reindeer herds, and dog teams. His engravings were photographic in their detail, unlike any others. But he was also the complete artist of his day, creating sculpture and model boats from ivory as well. Yet, his fame rested primarily on portraiture, his faithful rendition of photographs in ivory, many examples of which still exist in private and public collections. (Theodore Roosevelt in fig. 53 is an example.)

Since my 1955 meeting with Happy Jack's brother-in-law, Michael Kazingnuk, when I obtained my first information about this artist, we have now accumulated a large portfolio of his works to attest to his prodigious talent. But his personal life still has its mysteries, and

most of what we know about him has come from Kazingnuk. By 1955 Happy Jack had been dead for thirty-seven years (he died in the 1918 influenza epidemic). Old-timers of Nome remembered his name, and that he had been a famous ivory carver (what all Eskimo artists were called then), but they knew nothing about him as a man—a fate that befell so many Eskimos of the early days. A typical response was that of my old friend Charley Jones, who had known Happy Jack personally but had known nothing of his personal history. He was, he said, "just one of the many Eskimos who carved ivory."

I wrote about Happy Jack for the first time in *Artists of the Tundra and the Sea* (1961), and many years later, after I had learned more about his works, I brought Happy Jack up-to-date in two articles in *American Indian Art Magazine* (1984a, 1989). We will undoubtedly

Illus. 12. Happy Jack and his family. Nome, ca. 1908. Photograph by F. H. Nowell. Photograph courtesy of Caroline McLain Reader

find more of his works, but I doubt if we can learn any more about his personal life than I have already written. Even his birthdate is problematic, but it is thought that he was born about 1875 at Cape Nome, not far from future Nome. He lived on Little Diomede Island when a youth, and moved to Nome during the gold rush. He had at least two wives, two children (a son, who died, and a daughter), and a stepdaughter. His wife Assongy (Kazingnuk's sister) and his daughter also died of influenza in 1918 (illus. 12). No direct descendants survive.

Happy Jack: Tusk (figure 53)

Although I did not learn the details of Happy Jack's life until the summer of 1955, I had heard his name as the "best Eskimo artist," but I did not see any Happy Jack pieces during my museum research of 1954, nor did anyone in Nome have his works. I first saw a Happy Jack engraving in 1955, before I went to Nome for the summer. My museum research had caught the eye of Lucile McDonald, a feature writer, whose article about my research in *The Seattle Times* stirred the hopes of many readers who wanted to sell their ivory collections (McDonald 1954). My phone rang off the hook, and with all those opportunities, I rather regretted having turned down Polet's offer to buy his shop, but it was too late. I looked at some of the collections, but for the most part they contained duplicates of objects that I had already seen, though none by Happy Jack. I was in for a surprise, however, early in 1955, when a young man appeared unannounced at my door with a tusk wrapped in a newspaper—a gift from a Bremerton woman who wanted me to have it as an aid to my studies! This tusk (fig. 53 A, B) was engraved with figures only at the basal end, which are to be viewed with the tusk placed in a vertical, not a horizontal, position. Theodore Roosevelt on one side, under an eagle clutching an American flag, and on the opposite side, a prospector panning for gold.

Happy Jack engraved this tusk in the Nome city jail, where at times he was given a warm place to do his carving and engraving, or sometimes to sleep off the effects of a night on the town. I have not seen another Eskimo work of this kind, which, as Stuart Frank, director of the Kendall Whaling Museum in Sharon, Massachusetts, has reminded me, is reminiscent of the way Yankee whalers engraved walrus tusks. It is possible that Happy Jack encountered this idea when he went to San Francisco on a whaling ship in the 1890s. The tusk can be suspended from a hole in the tip end, which

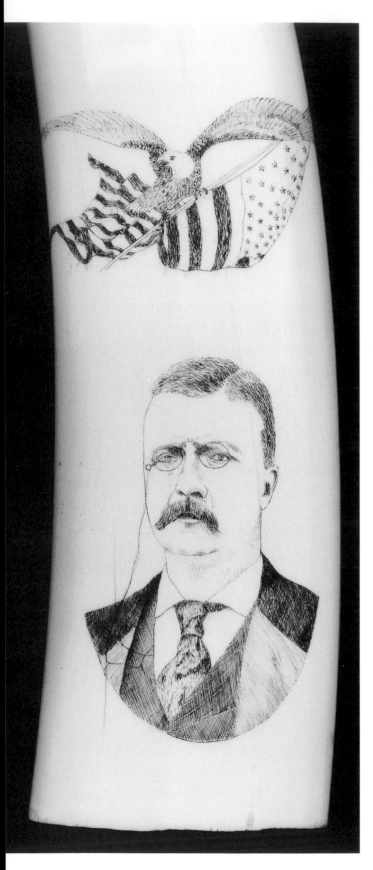

Fig. 53. Happy Jack, Nome. Walrus ivory tusk. A and B: reverse details shown. Engraved portraits of Theodore Roosevelt and a prospector. About 1915. 22″

was probably not originally drilled for the purpose of hanging, but for tying together in bunches by the Eskimo traders, a long-time practice before the gold rush. Tusks tied together in this way are depicted in nineteenth-century engravings from Little Diomede and Big Diomede islands, but holes were rarely found in tusks after souvenir engraving on whole tusks got a good start in Nome. For that reason, and because Roosevelt began his presidency in 1901, this piece probably dates from Happy Jack's earliest days in Nome.

I saw my next Happy Jack engravings (that is, they were supposed to be by Happy Jack) when we moved to the Kenmore area, north of Seattle, in 1956. There, one of my neighbors, Mrs. Ralph Hawley, showed me a collection of pieces that her father, John Winslow, an employee of the Standard Oil Company, had purchased from Happy Jack in 1902. By 1956 I had seen only two illustrations of Happy Jack's work (plus my Theodore Roosevelt), and I was eagerly looking forward to a collection that had been bought directly from him. But what I saw in the collection puzzled me, because the work was unlike the exquisitely detailed, almost photographic work that I had already seen. Yet I had no reason to doubt the authenticity, since the name "Happy Jack"—a man almost forgotten, but still remembered far from Nome—had been attached to this collection for more than fifty years. Included in the collection were two cribbage boards, a napkin ring, and several small pieces, which I later illustrated in *Artists of the Tundra and the Sea.* I saw this collection at the beginning of my research into Eskimo art, and having little information about Happy Jack's work to go on at that time, took the history of the objects at face value. But on the basis of dozens of works by him that I have subsequently seen, I do not believe that these were made by Happy Jack. They are still a mystery to me. Of course, a man as talented as he could have altered his engraving style, but I doubt that he would have produced the stiff dogs, for example, portrayed on the cribbage board. (These pieces are illustrated in Ray 1961: figs. 54–56; Ray 1984a: figs. 25, 26; Ray 1989: fig. 5.)

If Happy Jack did not make these pieces, he undoubtedly sold them, since his name was attached to them. Kazingnuk told me that Happy Jack sometimes had a sort of "school," where he helped carvers with their work, and he would peddle ivories on the street for men who could not speak English or who were not good traders. I have seen other collections that were purchased directly from Happy Jack which also contained suspect pieces. Such a purchase is no guarantee that the work was done by Happy Jack, and it should not be the basis for identification.

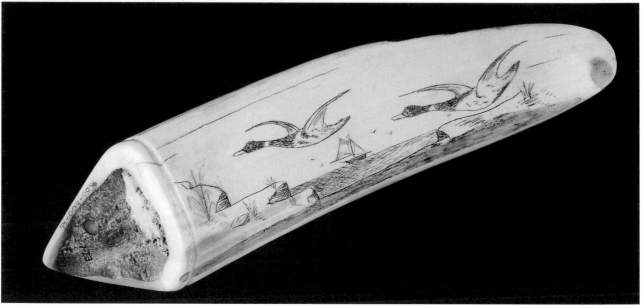

Happy Jack: Mattock (figure 54)

My next acquisition was a fairly small piece, which I purchased in 1964 from a Seattle dealer who had read about Happy Jack in *Artists of the Tundra and the Sea*. It was an important piece for me because it was only the second one I had seen with Happy Jack's signature. The first was a facsimile of a "Packer's Tar Soap" wrapper in the Historical Museum at Mystic Seaport, Connecticut. In that piece, Happy Jack had cut off the brown patina of an old ivory mattock, exposing a white soaplike surface on which he engraved the lovely

Fig. 54. Happy Jack, Nome. Walrus ivory mattock head. A and B: reverse sides shown. Engraved with a fox and a rabbit on one side; flying geese on the other. Before 1918. 9¾"

Packer's Tar Soap woman, shown with long tresses in a frame of pine branches, and the phrases "Pure as the Pines" and "Its Uses and how to use it." On the narrow edge he had engraved: "Made by Eskimo Happy Jack Nome, Alaska." (This piece is illustrated in Ray 1961: fig. 53; and Ray 1984a: fig. 8.)

The ivory on one end of my new acquisition (also an ivory mattock) was discolored brown before Happy Jack began engraving, because he outlined the inside edge of it with black, utilizing only the white portion of the ivory for a determined fox chasing a white rabbit amid some tufts of grass. This piece is a good example of both the delicate and heavy engraving that Happy Jack sometimes used on the same piece. The fox (54A), with his fierce energy in chasing the rabbit, is engraved with heavy, black strokes, whereas the geese flying over the water on the opposite side (54B) are drawn as lightly as their flight. Happy Jack's portraits were executed with decisive engraving—there was no hesitant mark. Theodore Roosevelt in figure 53A is heavily engraved; the prospector on the opposite side is engraved with much lighter marks. This dichotomy is also apparent in other pieces illustrating one of my articles about Happy Jack (see Ray 1984a: figs. 9, 13, and 14).

Happy Jack: Cribbage Board 1 (figure 55)

This small cribbage board is signed by Happy Jack, but it differs from his other pieces in this collection by his use of geometric designs and mountains as dominant themes on the top cribbage surface. To my knowledge, Happy Jack was the only artist who engraved such sumptuous mountains, and he made the most of

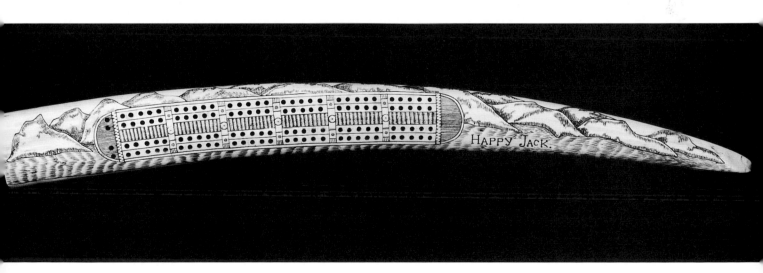

them on this piece, extending them the entire length. Someone is sure to question—perhaps after seeing a typical view of Nome from the sea—whether Happy Jack really saw such mountains. Happy Jack often visited the interior of Seward Peninsula, where he could see the beautiful Kigluiak Mountains to the northeast, and the Bendeleben Mountains near Norton Sound.

The animals on the reverse side have the limp quality that characterizes many of his bears and other animals. As usual, he outlines the mountains, the animals, and the ice floes with a deep cut but uses shallow cuts for fill-in. The ivory has turned a light cream color.

Happy Jack: Cribbage Board 2 (figure 56)

In 1991 I had the opportunity to buy three outstanding tusks, including a cribbage board that was unusual in two respects: it was a duplicate of one in the Museum of History and Industry in Seattle, which was dated 1915 by Mrs. Carl Lomen, who donated it to the museum; and it was unfinished. Happy Jack had been persuaded to part with it before he had drilled the holes on the top (fig. 56A) and before filling in the animals on the reverse side (fig. 56B). Outlines of the animals on that side are deeply incised, and it occurred to me that Happy Jack had used the same pattern for this cribbage board and the one in the museum, which I had illustrated in my two articles about him (Ray 1984a: figs. 19–21; and Ray 1989: figs. 15, 16). Thereupon, I asked Lois Rayne Bark of the museum to measure the figures for me. Sure enough, they were exactly the same size as in this cribbage board.

But there was another surprise. Iris Magnell, a serious collector of antique Alaskan postcards and photographs, who had seen the tusk, sent me a postcard of a dog team entitled *Howling Dog Team,* by F. H. Nowell, 1906, which she thought might be the model for one of the dog teams, and it was: for the team on the left tip end of the cribbage side (see illus. 13). On a later visit to Port Townsend, she brought another surprise, a postcard with several reindeer and herders, *Eskimo and their Reindeer, Alaska,* also by Nowell, which was the model for the group on the right end of this same cribbage board (illus. 14). Although both postcards are in color, they undoubtedly were hand-colored from original black-and-white photos.

Happy Jack faithfully copied the photographs with only minor alterations: he eliminated a man standing near the front of the dog team, no doubt because he was too tall for the narrow end, and, for balance, he added two dogs lying down at the front of the team (fig.

Fig. 56. Happy Jack, Nome. Cribbage board. A, B, and C: reverse sides and detail shown. Walrus ivory tusk with engraved scenes of dog team, reindeer herd, ptarmigans, and polar bear hunting walrus. About 1915. 30½"

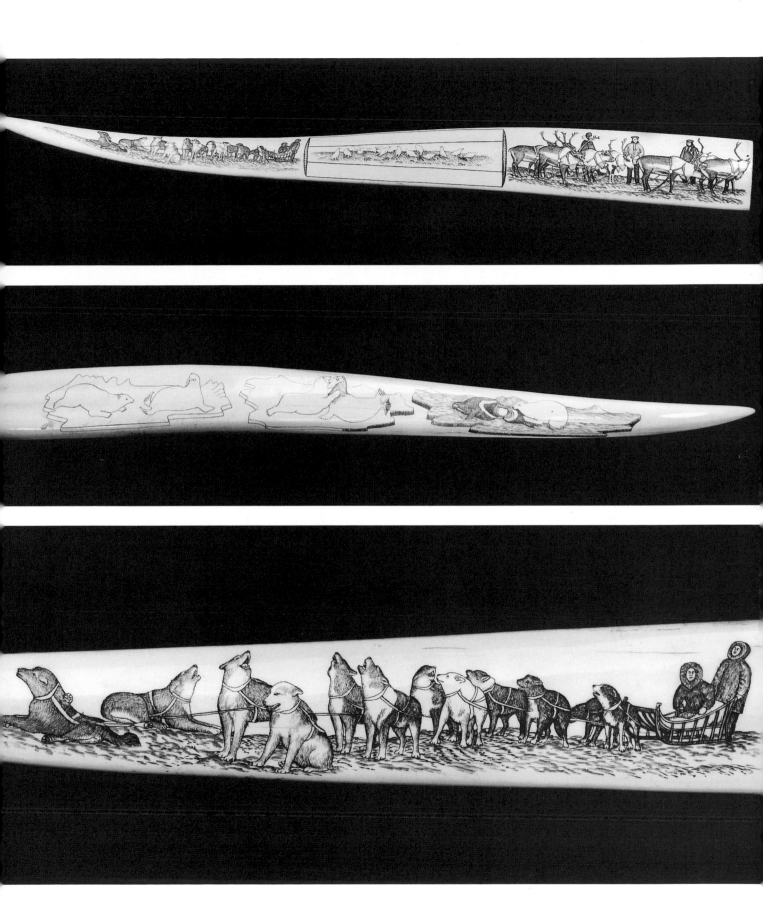

1999 — HOWLING DOG TEAM.

Copyright by F. H. Nowell, June 1906

Eskimo and their Reindeer, Alaska.

Illus. 13. *Howling Dog Team.* Old postcard. 1906. Photograph by F. H. Nowell. This was the model for the dog team on the tip end of a Happy Jack cribbage board (fig. 56). Iris Magnell collection

Illus. 14. *Eskimo and their Reindeer, Alaska.* Old postcard. This photograph by F. H. Nowell was the model for the engraving on a Happy Jack cribbage board (fig. 56). Iris Magnell collection

56C). On the other image, the reindeer antlers differ somewhat from the Nowell photograph. It is interesting to compare the slight differences in antlers on the cribbage board in the Museum of History and Industry with this one. Happy Jack followed the photograph almost exactly on the museum's cribbage board but added several antlers on this one. (See illustrations in Ray 1984a and 1989.)

This is a superb tusk, even though unfinished, which illustrates two of the most popular activities of Nome life during the 1910s—the running of dog teams, and reindeer herding. The howling dog team takes up one-third of the tip end of the top face, and the harnessed reindeer with three herders at the extreme right, another third; between them, where the cribbage holes should be, is a flock of eleven ptarmigan. On the unfinished reverse side, we see the steps taken by a polar bear to catch a meal (left to right): a bear is ready to attack a walrus on an ice floe; a bear kills the walrus; and a bear eats the walrus.

Dog Teams and Reindeer Herds

In the days before airplanes and snowmobiles, people in Alaska depended on dog teams and reindeer for transportation. Prospectors, traders, and miners eagerly adopted Eskimo dog-team travel for carrying passengers, freight, and mail, as well as for racing. Writing for the *Washington Star* in 1916, journalist Frank G. Carpenter said that "the whole of the interior [of Alaska] is dependent upon dogs for its winter transportation," and in Nome, dog team races were the highlights of the winter (Carpenter 1916).

After the excitement of the gold rush had subsided and Nome had become a town with a stable economy and an active social life, a few men organized the Nome Kennel Club in 1907 for the purpose of furthering interest in breeding better dogs, both for commercial use and for the small dog team races that had been held. Dog team racing came into the big time when, in the first week of April the next year, the first All-Alaska Sweepstakes race was run. This race, from Nome to Candle and back, a distance of 408 miles, was the favorite event of the year until 1917, after which it was not run because of World War I. People looked forward to it all year. Thousands of dollars were wagered, and winners were looked upon as heroes. (A first-hand description of these races was written by A. A. "Scotty" Allan, the famous dog musher, who owned the equally famous dog, "Baldy of Nome." See *Gold, Men and Dogs*, 1931, pp. 176–232.) Happy Jack had his pick of many dog team pictures, for they were a favorite subject for photographers. Probably all of Happy Jack's dog teams in ivory are specific teams from photographs or postcards.

These years were also euphoric in the reindeer industry, when the people administering the herds had visions of great commercial potential—as a food substitute for beef, and as transportation. The herding of domestic reindeer began in 1892, when Sheldon Jackson brought the first deer from Siberia to a place that he called Teller Reindeer Station on Port Clarence. On his two prior trips to northern Alaska in the revenue cutter *Bear,* Jackson was appalled at the sight of a bleak tundra and underground dwellings that looked more like huge gopher holes than homes, since he had come from the comfortable temperate zone of woodlands, meadows, and bustling cities. But the houses were warm and cozy, and the Eskimos lived very well on walrus, seals, fish, caribou, berries, and greens. Nevertheless, Jackson jumped to the conclusion that the people were starving, and he brought reindeer from Siberia every year from 1892 until 1902. The total of 1,280 deer formed the basis for future herds, including those of today. Administration of the various herds was under the Reindeer Service, a special department of the U.S. Bureau of Education. The reindeer were supposedly imported for the exclusive use of the Eskimos, but after several years, only a few Eskimos owned deer outright (the reindeer were in government and school herds) and herds had been loaned to Laplanders (the Saami, who had been imported to teach herding to the Eskimos) and to various missions. In 1914, the importing of reindeer deviated even further from its original purpose when the Lomen Corporation, a white business organization, purchased reindeer from herds owned by the Saami (the name preferred by Laplanders today) and two missions.

By this time there were many herds, some as far south as the Kuskokwim River, and with white owners looming as competitors to the Eskimos, William T. (Tom) Lopp and Walter Shields, administrators of the U.S. Bureau of Education in northwest Alaska, suggested that reindeer fairs be held to promote better herd management among Native owners. Consequently, the first of three fairs was held at the village of Marys Igloo in 1915 (another was organized in Akiak on the Kuskokwim River), in which techniques of herding and products management were discussed. There were also competitions to show Eskimo mastery of the animals: lasso contests, races, harness shows, sled shows, pulling contests, and exhibits of reindeer-skin clothing. Although the photograph of the herders and their reindeer probably dates from 1906 (as does the dog team), it is possible that the Lomens commissioned Happy Jack to make the cribbage board now in the Museum of History and Industry (and, subsequently, this one) after the 1915 fair. (Carl Lomen describes the fairs in his book, *Fifty Years in Alaska*.)

Happy Jack: Tusk (figure 57)

This tusk has three dog teams on one side and a herd of reindeer on the other. Near the herd, an Eskimo herder sits in a sled, and four other people are standing (one woman and three men), all of whom appear to be Saami. Training reindeer to pull sleds was one of the programs during the reindeer fairs, and many letters and reminiscences from this era tell of the exhilarating, and sometimes dangerous, experiences of reindeer driving. In the long run, though, using reindeer for transportation proved impractical because of their lack of stamina as well as problems of providing adequate forage on long trips. The dog teams, so carefully portrayed by Happy Jack on the opposite side of this tusk, proved superior in every way. The far-left dog team was copied from a photograph taken by B. B. Dobbs, *Milton Weil with his Malamute chorus, Nome Alaska* (illus. 15), which Iris Magnell also identified for me.

Illus. 15. *Milton Weil with his Malamute chorus, Nome Alaska.* Photograph by B. B. Dobbs. This is the model for a dog team on a Happy Jack tusk (fig. 57). Courtesy of L. Denny Collection, Archives, Alaska and Polar Regions Dept., University of Alaska Fairbanks, acc. no. 67-34-67

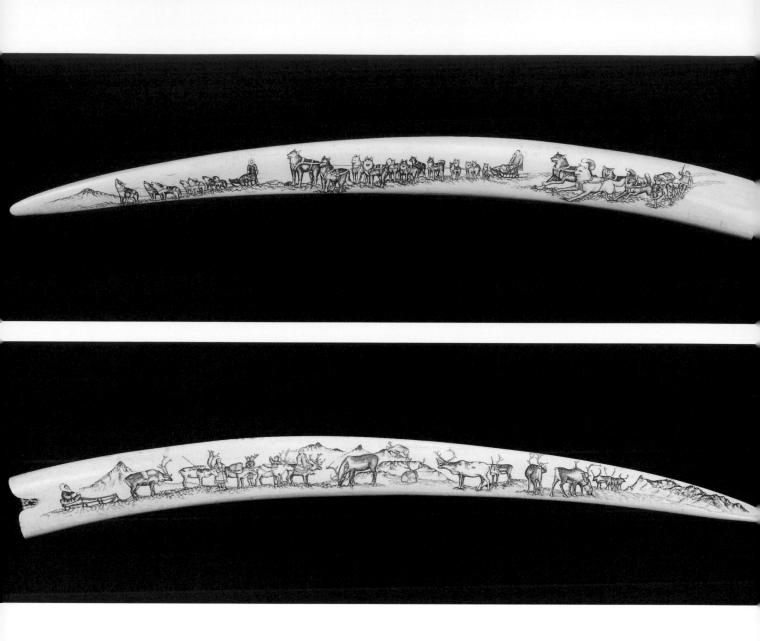

Happy Jack: Tusk (figure 58)

The third tusk in this series departs from the local subjects of dog teams and reindeer herds engraved on the other two with scenes quite foreign to the Nome area of that time. Happy Jack copied illustrations of what appear to be moose on one side and a commercial whaling scene on the other side of this 23-inch tusk. There were no moose on Seward Peninsula during the early twentieth century, nor was there commercial whaling with a sailing vessel within sight of the Nome coast. Happy Jack, however, did add a local touch to the moose scene—a fox stalking some ptarmigan at the tip end—apparently to balance the scene.

Fig. 57. Happy Jack, Nome. Walrus ivory tusk. A and B: reverse sides shown. Engraved scenes of dog team, reindeer herd. About 1915. 25½″

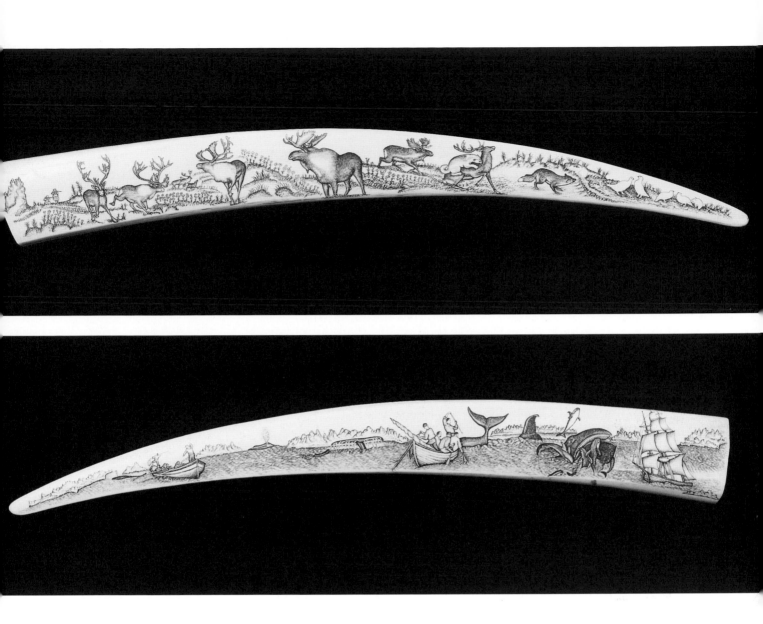

Fig. 58. Happy Jack, Nome. Walrus ivory tusk. A and B: reverse sides shown. Engraved moose on one side; commercial whaling scene on reverse. About 1915. 23″

This remarkable tusk is one of the strangest of all of Happy Jack's engravings that I have seen. The whaling scene conveys a more explosive character than is usual in his engravings, and the moose composition has a sort of yin-and-yang quality: two hunters near a rugged hill and a charging dog agitate the moose on the left, in contrast to the peaceful ptarmigan, unaware of the wily fox on the right; and the rigid rows of flowers (a new kind of plant on a Happy Jack piece) against the turmoil of the moose, in contrast to the wispy grass where the ptarmigan are feeding.

The commercial whaling scene is one that was never observed in the Nome area, even in the days of sailing ships which effectively ended in 1880, when the first steam whaler, *Mary and Helen,*

129

returned to San Francisco with one of the largest catches of oil and baleen in Arctic commercial fishing (Bockstoce 1986:210). This dramatic scene, with many of the figures out of scale, is without doubt a composite of several illustrations. In any event, Happy Jack included enough whales to have made the voyage of this vessel a lucrative one.

Engraved Ivory, 1918–1950

The influenza epidemic, which began in October 1918 in Nome, dealt a blow to ivory art with the death of many of the artists, including Happy Jack. Of an estimated 250 Eskimos who lived in Nome, 200 died, according to Carl Lomen (Cole 1984:136, from the Lomen Collection in the University of Alaska Fairbanks Archives).[2]

Happy Jack and other early-day artists made figurines and other three-dimensional objects as well as engravings, but after the 1918 epidemic, the art of engraving limped along with only a few high points until recently. Sculpture (always called "carving" at Nome) began to blossom, and with advice from collectors and dealers, ivory products had flooded the gift shops by the time I arrived in Nome in 1945: huge supplies of ivory figurines—birds, walrus, bears, and whales—ivory jewelry such as beads, brooches, and bracelets; buttons, gavels, chess sets, candlesticks, pickle forks, letter openers, carving sets, steak knives, and butter spreaders. There were few large engraved tusks or cribbage boards, although some were made with small carvings sitting atop them. Several King Island men engraved cribbage boards, but the work was rather rigid and unimaginative, and most of their engraving was done on smaller objects. The cribbage board was losing its popularity.

Billy Komonaseak: Cribbage Board (figure 59)

Billy Komonaseak of Wales (illus.16), who died in Nome in December 1943, was one of the better engravers of the post-1918 era. Like many artists, he did not vary his output once he had achieved success, and this cribbage board is similar to five others that I have seen, but is the only one with his name on it (fig.59B). All have a reindeer pulling a sled, with another reindeer trotting behind. And in different positions on the tusk, there are always seals, bears, and rabbits. The reindeer and sled were a bit of nostalgia, because by the 1940s the use of reindeer as draft animals was almost a thing of the

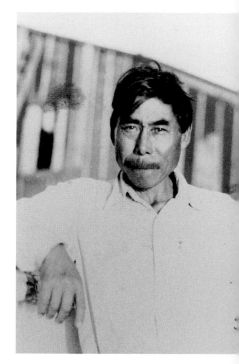

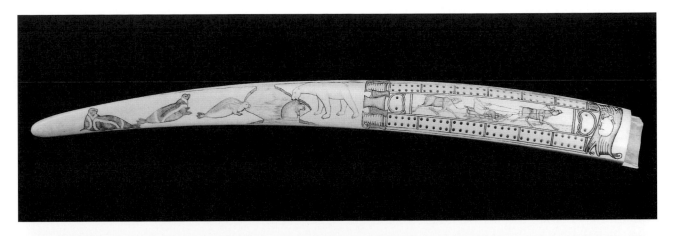

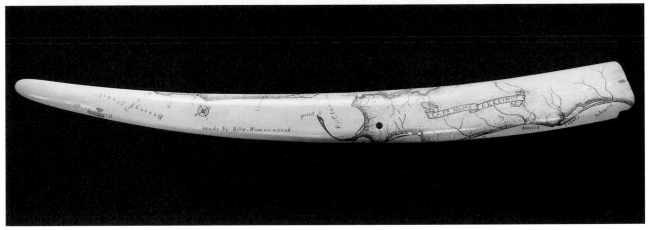

Illus. 16. Billy Komonoseak. Photograph courtesy of Frieda Larsen, who is Komonoseak's daughter, and Kathleen Lopp Smith

Fig. 59. Billy Komonaseak, Wales. Cribbage board. A and B: reverse sides shown. Walrus ivory tusk engraved with his signature reindeer and sled; map on reverse. About 1940. 26"

past (although, during a fair in Nome in April 1947, a reindeer and sled, such as this one, were featured in a parade).

Billy Komonaseak grew up in an unusual environment (Cape Prince of Wales) where the old customs were strictly adhered to, but where his people, known throughout the Bering Strait area as aggressive and independent, accepted the new culture of western education with greater fervor than was shown in many Alaskan villages. The school at Wales, first established in 1890 by Tom Lopp and Harrison R. Thornton, stood out as a model through difficult days ahead for both teachers and pupils. Not only did the Wales pupils learn basic literacy but they were encouraged to indulge their natural talent for drawing.[3] Billy was one of four bright lads who were trained at Wales to become teachers, and indeed, two of them, Arthur Nagozruk, Sr., and Charles Menadelook, did go on to distinguished careers as the first Native teachers in western Alaska (Adlooat Sowle, a third teacher, died young). But Billy (who had originally been given the name Jerry!) had to drop out of school because he was needed at home. His education is evident in the map on the reverse side of this cribbage board (fig. 59B) because, unlike the misspelled words on the other maps, all of his names are correct. He also had an interest in maps and the sea, for he worked on boats, including the SS *Cordova* under Captain S. T. L. Whitlam. Besides his cribbage boards, Komonaseak was noted for making billikens with unusual facial expressions, which prompted Whitlam to call him "Billiken." Hence, his first name, Billy; and the use of Billiken sometimes as an alternate surname for his family.[4]

Engraved Ivory: 1950–1970

The 1930s and 1940s saw the emergence of a different kind of graphic art with the use of reindeer skin and paper by self-taught artists such as George Ahgupuk, Florence Malewotkuk, Robert Mayokok, Kivetoruk Moses, and Wilbur Walluk. In the 1960s and 1970s, printmakers such as Bernard Katexac, Peter J. Seeganna, Joseph Senungetuk, and many others made multicolor prints in formal classes and workshops. With the growing popularity of the new graphic art and a decreasing supply of ivory, engraving on ivory took a back seat. Very few whole tusks were engraved as in the heyday of that art prior to the 1918 influenza epidemic, and engraving was usually confined to an animal figure, a simple hunting scene, or geometric designs. The majority of engraved objects were small, such as the cribbage board in figure 60 and the book marker and letter opener in figure 61.

John Killarzoac: Cribbage Board (figure 60)

The small ivory cribbage board, only 7½ inches long, is an ideal pocket-size for a perambulating cribbage player. Made by John Killarzoac of King Island in 1961, the designs, though simple and unimaginative, are neat and well executed.

Ivory Book Marker and Letter Opener; Walrus-Tooth Watch Fobs (figure 61)

The engravings on the book marker and letter opener, both made of mammoth ivory, are imprecise. I bought these pieces at King Island Village, west of Nome, but the work is so poor (the Eskimo woman on the book marker, and the seal on the letter opener) that no one

Fig. 60. John Killarzoac, King Island. Cribbage board. Walrus ivory. 1961. 7½"

Fig. 61. Anonymous, Nome. Letter opener (7½") and book marker (4⅛") made of mammoth ivory. 1950. Anonymous, King Island. Watch fobs (2") made of walrus tooth. 1968

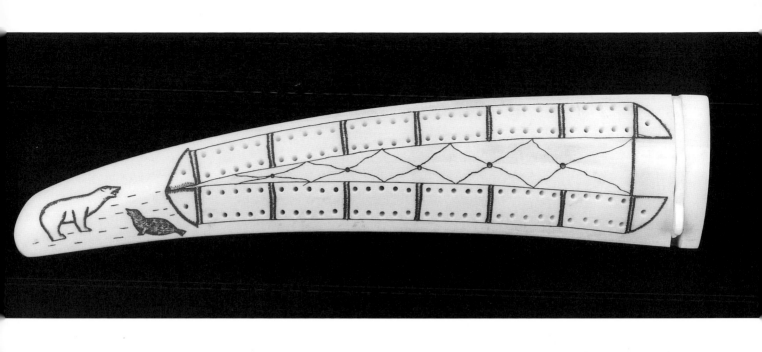

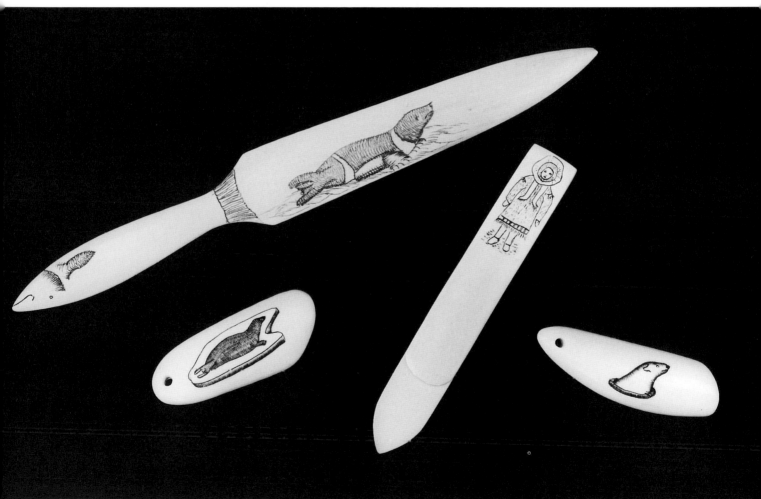

133

would give me the names of the persons who had made them. I suspect that they were the work of beginners.

The ANAC catalog of 1973 illustrated a number of engraved walrus teeth and sperm whale teeth with no indication as to their place of origin, but probably they came from King Island. Although these pieces are described in the catalog as being "Similar to the Scrimshaw of Whaling Times," only two of the twenty-eight pieces have sailing ships. The rest of the scenes feature typically Eskimo motifs: a single bird, walrus, or seal, and a two-figure scene of a hunter after a polar bear or a whale (ANAC, 1973, p. 19).

The two walrus teeth in figure 61, each only two inches long, are similar to the ones illustrated in the ANAC catalog. The use of such tiny objects as a medium (as well as mammoth ivory, which was dug from the ground and was sometimes crumbly) reflected the increasing difficulty of getting materials for carving, even in Alaska, especially for carvers who were not hunters or who had no friends or relatives who hunted walrus. The vignettes on these two pendants— a figure of a seal on an ice cake on one side and a seal's head rising from the water on the other—have been engraved by the hundreds, sometimes by the best engravers, for a bit of income in an area where prices have always been high.

Andy Tingook: 8-link Bracelet; Earrings (figure 62)

One of the interesting departures from the run-of-the-mill engraving during the 1950s and 1960s was the work of Andrew Tingook (illus. 17), a man from Shishmaref who lived in Nome and preferred to be called "Andy." In the 1940s I had bought a so-called story bracelet, six ivory links strung together with elasticized thread which told a rather unidentifiable "story"—an umiak under sail, a round summer tent, a walrus, a whale, a polar bear and a seal— made by an unidentified artist from Shishmaref (fig. 62; 6-links).

When I returned to Nome in 1955 for a study of ivory carving, I saw another story bracelet (fig. 62, 8 links) a work of great quality by Tingook. His engraving on the tiny links (⅝" by ¹¹⁄₁₆") was far superior to the work that was characteristic of the local engraving on any kind of object, and it really told a story. His story in eight links had a logical sequence: (1) a hunter heads out to sea to hunt seals in his kayak; (2) the hunter stands; (3) the hunter walks; (4) the hunter lies prone with a rifle, shooting at a seal, which is link number 5; (6) the hunter pulls the seal home; (7) his wife cuts up the seal; and (8) his wife dries the meat on a rack. The earrings that he made to match

Fig. 62. Andy Tingook, Shishmaref. Eight-link "story bracelet" and matching earrings. Walrus ivory. 1955. Links ⅝" by ¹¹⁄₁₆"; earrings ¹¹⁄₁₆" square. Anonymous, Shishmaref. Six-link bracelet. White walrus ivory and brown old ivory, elastic thread. 1946. Each white link ½" by ¾"

Illus. 17. Andy Tingook. Nome 1973. Photograph by Dennis Corrington

the bracelet are of the standing hunter (link 2) and his wife cutting up the seal (link 7).

Shishmaref did not have a souvenir-carving tradition, as did the Nome area and the islands in the Bering Strait, so I was curious as to the origin of these bracelets. I learned from Edward Keithahn, former director of the Alaska State Museum, that Tingook and his brothers had themselves come up with the idea of the story bracelet in the 1920s, while Keithahn and his wife were teaching in Shishmaref. The first bracelets were like the one with the unrelated subjects that I had purchased in 1946, but Andy had developed the classic story bracelet with his extremely fine engraving: the woman cutting up the seal in link 7 is only ⅜ inches high. Although he used a magnifying glass while engraving, the small size is remarkable because his eyesight was failing in 1955 at age fifty-seven. Yet even in 1973, when he was almost blind, Andy was still making his bracelets.

Engraved Ivory, 1990s

In recent years the subject matter of ivory engraving had become unimaginative and pedestrian, and the technique also was rather poor, but in 1990 and 1991, I became aware for the first time of some unusually fine engraving by two men—Alvin Aningayou of St. Lawrence Island, and Frank Miller of Teller.

Alvin Aningayou (figure 63)

Alvin made the piece in this collection in 1991, when he was twenty-two years old. I bought it at the Ivory Broker in Anchorage. The engraving of four vignettes on an old ivory tool with a tan patina is the most delicate workmanship I've encountered since Happy Jack's; in fact, this is even finer. Except for outlines, Happy Jack's incisions cannot be felt by the finger but are perceptible with the fingernail. Aningayou's engraving cannot be felt even with the fingernail. This piece looks and feels like a glossy photograph, yet I was told that the work had been done with dental tools.

The subject matter is mystifying since the costumes and dog team portrayed are not Alaskan. Alvin apparently copied romanticized illustrations from an early-day adventure publication, probably

Fig. 63. Alvin Aningayou, St. Lawrence Island. Engraving on an old ivory tool. Mounted on wooden base. 1991. Length 10¼"

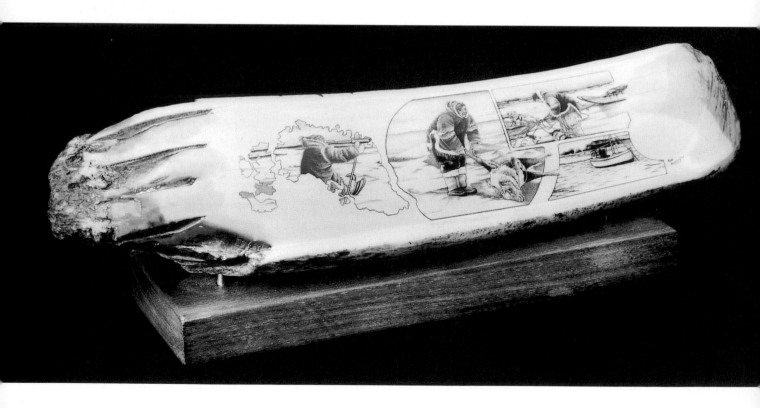

Canadian, perhaps Siberian Eskimo. The pictures are (from left to right): (1) a man looking through a telescope superimposed on what looks like a map of islands in the Canadian Arctic; (2) a man with a dead reindeer or caribou; (3) a man harnessing his dogs in fan pattern, which is the Canadian method—the Alaskan harnessing pattern is in tandem—and behind him is a strangely shaped sled with solid wood sides; and (4) below this vignette is a white man's sloop.

Frank Miller (figure 64)

Frank Miller's engraving of a man in winter clothing is on a thin cross-section of a walrus tusk which was given to me by Iris Magnell, who bought it in Teller in 1990. The engraving is almost as fine as Aningayou's—the incisions are slightly felt with the fingernail—but the figure does not look so much like a photograph as Aningayou's, and it has a greater feeling of spontaneity.

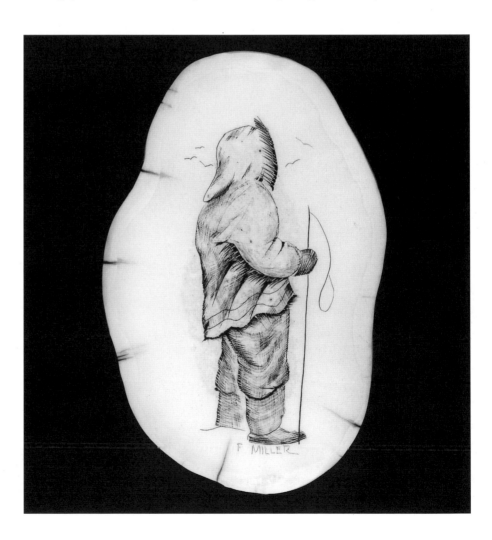

Fig. 64. Frank Miller, Teller. Engraving on a slice of walrus tusk. 1990. Height 2⁷⁄₁₉″

Canadian Inuit Art

Canadian Eskimo art, or Inuit art as it is now commonly called, has had a history quite different from that of Alaskan Eskimos. Alaskan Eskimo art has roots dating back more than two thousand years in the sculpture and decorative designs of the early cultures—called Okvik, Old Bering Sea, Punuk, Ipiutak, and Thule—each with its own style of art and continuing unbroken, though with changes, until the present day. The Canadians have had no such obvious continuum, although there is evidence of unusual art in scattered archeological sites; and although not much attention has been paid to their "tourist art," articles of ivory, stone, and fur were made for sale here and there whenever explorers or traders visited their isolated villages.

In Alaska, by contrast, huge collections of Eskimo objects of all materials were made by collectors and explorers to Alaska, and from the arrival of the first Europeans in the Aleutian Islands and on the coast to the north, the Eskimos diligently set to work making mementos. Some of the earliest souvenirs were boat and sled models, basketry, and ivory figurines and engravings. Ivory, especially, defined Alaskan Eskimo art because of the preponderance of walrus herds, which migrated through the Bering Strait in great numbers. Canadian ivory carvings were comparatively scarce and almost unknown to the wider world.

This situation changed, however, during the early 1950s when Inuit stone carvings, and some ivory, went to market by the thousands. All of a sudden, it seemed, Eskimo art became synonymous with that of Canada. This unusual turn of events began in 1948 when James A. Houston, an artist on a painting trip, visited the settlement of Port Harrison on the shore of Hudson Bay. He became interested in small stone carvings, and on his return to Montreal he showed his collection to members of the Canadian Handicrafts Guild. Then, according to Houston, the Guild began a "test purchase" in 1949 as a means of helping the Eskimos economically. When he advised the people at Port Harrison, Povungnituk, and Cape Smith that he would buy their handicrafts, "the place became a veritable hive of activity . . . and they gladly devoted much of their time and interest to their new industry . . . and the Eskimos in all three of the places visited were enthusiastically creating before the trip had ended." Houston returned to Montreal with about "a thousand articles." In November 1949, a sale held by the Guild was sold out within three days.

In 1950, with the success of the sale, Houston returned to the Port Harrison–Povungnituk area and also to Repulse Bay, where "a satisfactory beginning was made." Here, there was a larger percentage of ivory work than in the area farther south. By 1952, Houston reported that five trips had been made, and twenty thousand pieces had been collected and sold by the Guild. "The supply has not begun to meet the demand" (Swinton 1972:123–24).[1]

During these early years of collecting and presenting commercial incentives to the villagers, the Canadian Handicrafts Guild issued a small manual written and illustrated by Houston "to encourage [the Eskimos] in their native arts. It is hoped that these illustrations will suggest to them some of their objects which are useful and acceptable to the white man." These included kayak models, animal figurines, human figurines in typical Eskimo garb, slippers, mittens, purses, baskets, knife and ulu handles, cribbage boards—even a totem pole!—(Houston 1951). According to George Rogers and Danny Pierce, writing in an art study commissioned by the University of Alaska, it was soon realized that such direction would "snuff out creativity," and with the danger "almost immediately recognized," the manuals were recalled and destroyed (University of Alaska 1964:86) But according to George Swinton, the booklet was used to a limited extent, although it never reached "far beyond Ungava. I could find traces of it only in Port Harrison, Povungnituk, and Ottawa—and it was withdrawn from circulation and even office use before the middle fifties" (Swinton 1972:131, 133).[2]

In the 1990s Canadian "Inuit art" is more familiar to the average person than is Alaskan Eskimo art. Today the difference between

Alaskan and Canadian Eskimo art production is striking. On the one hand, Canadian artists work under the umbrella of village names that have become recognizable, and famous, for their work; for example, Baker Lake, Cape Dorset, Povungnituk. Individual artists are also well known, but their association with an economic organization and a well-oiled village publicity brought them to the attention of buyers and collectors in the first place. In Alaska, on the other hand, there is no such organization along village lines nor any government effort to sell the art. Furthermore, Alaskan Eskimo artists are a variable lot, ranging from a few ivory carvers who have had a limited education and who speak little English to those who have their master's degree in fine arts and teach in universities. The one big organizational effort at marketing art through Alaska Native Arts and Crafts (ANAC) was of limited success, and ANAC became a private outlet in Anchorage; the Nome Skin Sewers Cooperative Association, as we have seen, had a specialized product, but could not continue; and several other organizations, such as Sunarit Associates, did not work out at all. In consequence, individual artists in Alaska must fend for themselves, and they sell to only a few galleries in Alaska and the other states. The younger Alaskan artists are moving into the mainstream of art with their large sculptures and canvases, and some are deliberately trying to eliminate the prefix of "Eskimo." All Eskimo artists of Canada are Inuit artists.

Because of the direction and encouragement given to the Canadian Inuit artist—or perhaps in spite of it—the art has blossomed in ways unimagined when the first little carvings were brought to the Guild. Accompanying all of this blossoming, an incredible and continual number of publications has brought this art to the attention of the public throughout the past four decades. I think that at least five times more articles, books, brochures, and pamphlets have been written and issued for Canadian art than for that of Alaska. Perhaps the difference is not so obvious in full-length books, but the quantity of pamphlets, calendars, booklets about the artists, and announcements of new editions of prints and new shipments of sculpture annually from the various villages to the many galleries in the world that specialize in Canadian art is overwhelming.[3]

Six Stone Carvings

The six carvings included in this collection date from the early 1950s and 1960s. All are small, in contrast to many of the huge pieces that have been made later. Three of them come from Port Harrison, the first village from which Houston made his collection.

The first three figures (a hunter, a bird, and two whales) date from 1952, and a bear, a few years later. These carvings, all made from black stone, arrived unannounced as a gift from two friends, Dorothy and Maurice Kamen-Kaye, a retired ethnobotanist and geologist respectively, living in Cambridge, Massachusetts. They had purchased all but the bear in Regina, Saskatchewan, in 1952 when the sculpture had first arrived there for sale. The bear was purchased in Montreal. When I unpacked them, my first thought (after recovering from my surprise) was how had they survived intact as they moved from place to place, because there were many fragile, removable parts to the pieces. Dorothy explained that whenever they moved, she put all of the separate pieces in sealed envelopes. And there are many little pieces: the hunter's spear and his knife and two removable ivory pegs that fasten him to the base; a removable ivory peg under each whale; and the removable pole that "flies" the bird above the base; and three tiny stone eggs in the nest. The eggs once had a narrow escape when, in the Kamen-Kayes' New York apartment, two little girls found the bird irresistible. After they had left, Dorothy saw that one of the eggs was missing, but a search turned up nothing. Her housekeeper, who came the next morning, vacuumed the rug and emptied the bag on a newspaper—and there was the egg!

Camp of Akeeaktashook: The Hunter (figure 65)

The hunter stands on an irregular shaped stone base. I think that the spear, the knife, and the pegs in the feet are ivory, although they are so sliverlike they might be bone. I did not know who had made these figurines until George Swinton, artist and Canadian Inuit art expert, identified them for me in 1993. (He was in Port Townsend, Washington—where I live—to give a slide lecture in conjunction with the opening of a new art gallery). Swinton said that the little hunter had been made in the camp of Akeeaktashook at Port Harrison, and in evaluating it, he pronounced it worthy of an "A-plus." Akeeaktashook later moved to Craig Harbour, Ellesmere Island, where he died in an accident in 1954.

This figure is very much like the drawing of a hunter on page 14 of the suppressed manual of 1951. Either this figurine was copied from the manual, or the manual illustration was copied from a Port Harrison carving. This hunter differs from the one in the manual by

holding a knife instead of a spear in his left hand, but a sculpture of a hunter on the cover of *Canadian Eskimo Art* (Houston 1954) is exactly like the drawing in the manual.

Camp of Akeeaktashook: Bird, Nest, and Three Eggs (figure 65)

The bird has a wing span of 3½ inches and is flying about 2 inches above the base. The nest is an oval depression scooped out of the base and has an elevated lip. Each little egg is only ⅜ inches long. George Swinton told me that this also was probably from the camp of Akeeaktashook, and he gave it a "B-plus."

Two Whales (figure 66)

The two whales were made by an unidentified carver, although this piece, made of stone similar to the hunter and the bird, may also be from Port Harrison. Apparently quite a few such pieces were made at that time, although Houston wrote in *Canadian Eskimo Art* that [the

Fig. 65. Camp of Akeeaktashook, Port Harrison, Canada. A: Hunter. Soapstone sculpture, with bone implements. About 1952. Height of man: 2⅞". B: Bird with three eggs in a nest. Soapstone sculpture with ivory pegs. About 1952. 3" from base to top.

Fig. 66. Anonymous, Canadian Inuit. A: Two whales. Soapstone. About 1952. Longer whale 4½"; B: Bear. Soapstone. About 1956. 5¾"

carver] is usually reluctant to copy or repeat a subject of his own, or indeed anybody else's work" (1954:27). I addressed this contradiction in my *Artists of the Tundra and the Sea,* since not only the Canadian artist, but Eskimo artists everywhere from time immemorial have made copies (1961:136). Both of the whales are pegged into a slab of stone with removable ivory pegs.

Bear (figure 66)

This bear was purchased about 1956 in a Montreal gallery. The carver has not been identified. Its stiff posture differs from that of the majority of bears, which were made in profusion in many unusual poses in most of the villages.

Celina Seeleenak: Bird (figure 67)

This bird of gray stone (fig. 67A) was my first piece of Canadian stone art. It was given to me by George Swinton in 1963 when he

discovered that we had similar interests, although Canada's Repulse Bay and Alaska lay several thousand miles apart.

Panniack Siusangnark: Woman (figure 67)

I bought this sculpture (fig. 67B) in Hamilton, Bermuda, in 1966. The facial features of this woman are well defined, but the arms hang at a strange angle. When I bought it I thought that the shape of the arms had been a carving error, but it apparently was a popular form, because I later saw illustrations of four similar figures, all from Repulse Bay, each by a different carver (Martijn 1967:16; Swinton 1972: fig. 775). The name "Susangnert" was written on the official Canadian sales form, but George Swinton has told me that the correct name should be Panniack Siusangnark. Possibly the figure may have been made by her husband, Paul, since authorship of Repulse Bay figures is sometimes difficult to distinguish (Swinton to author, 21 October 1994).

Fig. 67. A: Celina Seeleenak, Repulse Bay, Canada. Sculpture of a bird. Soapstone. 1963. Length 5"; B: Panniack Siusangnark, Repulse Bay, Canada. Sculpture of a woman. Soapstone. 1966. Height 4"

144   Canadian Inuit Art

Athabascan Chief's Coat

This coat (fig. 68) is the only Alaskan Athabascan piece that I have owned. It is from an area in which I have done little research, but I could not pass up the beautiful beadwork when it was offered for sale. Although I have kept up with the literature on Athabascan culture and history, I was unsure of its specific provenience, so I wrote to several experts in the field of Athabascan material culture. Ann Chandonnet, a writer who has had a long acquaintance with Athabascan people, and who has examined coats in museums, gave me helpful information. Adding her information to that which I already had, we have concluded that this coat was from the Tanana area (Chandonnet to author, 27 November 1989). A coat similar to this in style, fur, and beading is worn by Chief Charlie of Minto in photographs taken at the Tanana chiefs conference in Fairbanks in 1915, and also by a Tanana River man photographed in 1926 (Duncan 1989:149; McKennan 1981:574; Patty 1971:2, 6; VanStone 1974: cover).

This chief's coat is 35½ inches long and is well made of moose hide, with skillful beadwork of many colored seed beads. A fringe of beaver fur, 3 inches wide, edges each front opening, with a fringe 4 inches wide at the bottom of the coat and the sleeves. A strip of red flannel 2⅛ inches wide is sewed the entire length of the coat next to each front fur strip, affording the bright background for beaded designs of flowers and leaves. The flowers and "leaves" (kidney-shape and oval designs) are repeated four times in the following pattern: a six-petal flower of black and translucent rose beads with a

Fig. 68. Anonymous, probably
Tanana, Alaska. A. Chief's coat.
Tanned moose hide, felt cloth,
beads. 1920s or 1930s. Length
35½". B. Back yoke, detail

green center, and a green flower (and green center) of four petals.
Connecting all of them is a ropelike line made up of two rows of
black beads flanked by a row of translucent rose beads. This beaded
line has spurs made of three green beads set at right angles along its
entire length on both sides, except in eight places where the line
curves. Jutting from each curve are six spurs made up of three light-
blue beads tipped by two yellow ones. Opposite each of these curves
is a kidney-shape or oval design. A solid row of white seed beads,
sewed lengthwise, divides the flannel from a strip of old cloth, a
half-inch wide. The other side of the strip is also trimmed with
white seed beads in an intricate design made by each bead sewed
lengthwise, alternating with one sewed at right angles, or "zipper
edging."

The back yoke (fig. 68B), which is about 20 inches long by 6
inches wide, repeats the motifs of the front panels, also on red flannel: four of the six-petal translucent-rose flowers alternate with
three of the four-petal green flowers, all connected by strands of parallel rows of black and rose-color beads. If the yoke were divided
down the middle, each half would be equal. The oval and kidney-
shape designs have the following color schemes: yellow with black
center, light-blue with black center, green with white center, white
with green center, and black with rose center. A deerskin fringe of
pieces 3 inches by ¼ inch hangs from the sides and bottom of the
yoke and across the top seam of each sleeve.[1]

Although the coat has obviously been worn a lot, with a small
mend in the back and what appear to be two small burns on the left
sleeve, it is in excellent condition. The beadwork and fur look as
fresh as the day it was made.

Can This Be Eskimo Art?

When I first lived in Alaska in the 1940s, the shops of Anchorage, Juneau, and Nome had large inventories of Eskimo products, especially ivory carvings, fur mittens, mukluks, and parkas. Walrus ivory was in unrestricted use, fur animals were plentiful, and a huge demand for Eskimo-made things had developed during World War II wherever there were military installations. As I became better acquainted with the ivory carvings, I realized that some had a different look from those made at Bering Strait. I saw names like "Nunuk" and "Nuguruk" inscribed on pieces at a time when most ivory art was anonymous; few Eskimos in the Nome vicinity signed their work, and if they did, they used the binomial. No one could tell me who Nunuk or Nuguruk were, but someone told me that *nuguruk* meant "good."[1] I later learned that these objects were made in Seattle, usually mass-produced from a master copy by non-Eskimos in several manufacturing firms. Typical northern subjects were engraved on ivory pieces (usually elephant ivory, with a tag "genuine ivory"), which were then sent to Alaska, where customers mistakenly thought they were buying Eskimo-made objects of walrus ivory.

The Seattle Connection

One Seattle company was different. Porter and Johnson (later named Leonard F. Porter, Inc.), employed Alaskan Eskimos to design and engrave objects such as steak knife handles, book markers, and letter openers, and to make sculptures of animal and Eskimo figures. Among the Eskimo artists employed by Porter were Harry Apodruk and William Luke from White Mountain, Aloysius Ayac from King Island, Thomas Ekak from Wainwright, and Wilbur Walluk from Shishmaref. Porter encouraged his employees to invent original designs, which were occasionally hand-engraved but were more often copied and mass-produced by machine on elephant ivory.

Harry Apodruk, Thomas Ekak, Howard Rock, and Wilbur Walluk (figures 69–71)

All of these men were artists in their own right, and their employment in Seattle was an economic necessity. Wilbur Walluk had already produced pen-and-ink drawings and watercolors in Alaska before he began working at Porter's. One of Porter's most popular items was tableware with typical scenes of Eskimo life, most of which were designed by Wilbur Walluk until his death in 1968 at age forty. Sometimes Walluk signed his work, but not when someone else copied his designs on a pantograph, as in a set of six steak knives, illustrated in figure 69. Each handle has a different scene designed by Walluk and engraved by Harry Apodruk: five men in an umiak spearing a whale, ice floes and seals, moose in a forest, a dog team, four caribou, and walrus on an ice floe. All of the knife handles are made of elephant ivory and are quite yellowed, which suggests that they were artificially aged, but I had not discussed this with Porter.

By the 1960s the Seattle companies were using more elephant ivory than walrus ivory. The latter had been plentiful until it was banned, but the source of elephant ivory was also drying up, so Porter's company experimented with other materials, one of which was baleen (whalebone). Apodruk's letter opener of shiny black baleen with a vignette of contrasting white in figure 70 was one of the successful items.

Another artist, Howard Weyahok (Rock) of Point Hope, was employed in the 1940s by James L. Houston Manufacturing Company, but I do not know whether Houston ever employed other Eskimos. Rock, who had already made a name for himself as an artist in Seattle, was a student at the University of Washington in 1939 when he began working for Houston. He had been finding it difficult to make a living as an artist, and Houston proposed that he engrave Eskimo scenes for him, although Rock had never before

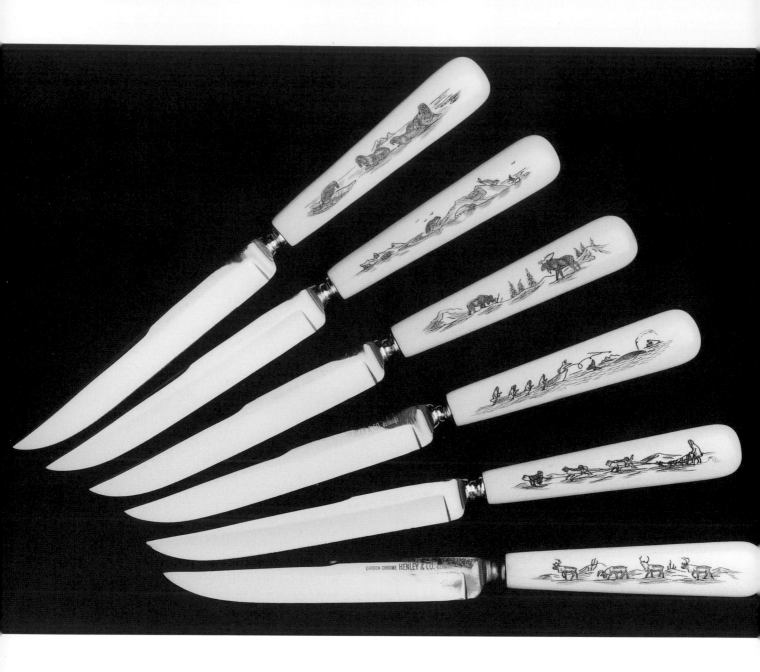

engraved ivory. Rock found it difficult going at first, but soon was proficient enough to work full time. He made as much as $200 a month early in 1940, and photographs of himself and his designs were advertised in gift-store windows. Yet despite his success, he did not enjoy the work. According to Lael Morgan, who wrote about Rock's commercial engraving in *Art and Eskimo Power* (1988), he personally engraved all of his pieces from his own designs, which was not always the case at the Porter company, as we have seen. An example of his work (fig. 70) is the cheese slicer handle, engraved on elephant ivory, with an idealized winter scene of an elevated log-

Fig. 69. Wilbur Walluk, Shishmaref, designer; Harry Apodruk, White Mountain, engraver, at Leonard Porter, Inc., Seattle. Steak knives. Engraved elephant ivory, stainless steel blades. 1960s. Length of handles 3¾"

Fig. 70. A: Harry Apodruk, White Mountain. Letter opener. Baleen. Made for Leonard F. Porter, Inc., Seattle. 1960s. 8⅓" B: Howard Weyahok (Rock), Point Hope. Handle for cheese slicer. Elephant ivory. Made for James L. Houston Mfg. Co., Seattle. 1940. Length of handle 2⅔"

storage cache in a conifer forest. Rock signed it "Howard Weyahok," *weyahok* meaning "rock" in Inupiaq.

Two of Thomas Ekak's figurines are included in this collection of Seattle commercial products. A standing bear and an Eskimo woman were made by him in 1959 or 1960 at Porter's establishment (fig. 71). They are made of sperm whale tooth (another material used by the Porter company) and are equal to anything made in the Nome area at that time. I have seen these sculptures in several collections, and when the owners learned that they had been made in Seattle instead of Alaska they were surprised and sometimes angry. They

had purchased them as Alaskan-made, and were not always mollified after they learned that they were indeed made by an Alaskan Eskimo.

    As these examples show, some of the objects made by Eskimos in the Seattle commercial establishments were equal in quality to any that were being made in Alaska at that time, yet most collectors feel they do not deserve a place on their shelves. This is a shame, because these pieces were made by men who would have been working in Alaska had they had the opportunity. Their works are in no sense fraudulent, unlike those that bore the names "Nunuk" or "Nuguruk" which were made by non-Eskimos in other manufacturing establishments, and which have brought no end of grief to customers (fig. 72). I have received numerous inquiries about these names from hapless buyers. A classic case (ca. 1960) involved an

Fig. 71. Thomas Ekak, Wainwright. Sculptures of a bear and a woman. Sperm whale teeth. Made for Leonard F. Porter, Inc., Seattle. 1960. Height of bear 3⅔"; height of woman 3⅓"

Fig. 72. Anonymous, Seattle. Brooch. Elephant ivory. Engraved and signed with fictional name "Nuguruk" on reverse. 1960s.

Alaskan shop owner who told a buyer that a barbecue set signed "Nunuk" was not only made in Alaska but was the last set the "Natives would be allowed to carve out of whole tusks." The dealer finally admitted that the set was made in Seattle.

One of the strangest stories in the Nunuk saga was from a man who wrote me for further information about Nunuk because "a young art student in the Juneau museum" had told him that Nunuk was "highly regarded and worked in the 1930s, and [another man said that he] has seen his work and believes Nunuk is from St. Lawrence" (Harold E. Haas to author, Santa Rosa, California, 4 August 1984).

I have spent more time than I like to admit looking at ivory in Alaskan shops since 1945, but during the 1970s I was most interested in the commercially made wares sold among the authentic objects, and how clerks responded to questions about them. It was generally a dismal procedure—most of the clerks either knew nothing about the ivory they were selling or else gave me false information. Several shops sold only authentic goods, but how could the tourists and souvenir hunters know which ones to trust? Eventually there were enough complaints from disgruntled artisans and customers to reach the office of the Federal Trade Commission, which viewed the making of objects by non-Eskimos and with non-Native materials as fraudulent practice.

The Federal Trade Commission, according to a news release of 12 March 1974, alleged that six Pacific Northwest firms misrepresented their products as handmade in Alaska by Alaskan Native Americans, whereas they were often made by non-Alaskans and on machines. The complaints were against five manufacturers and one wholesaler. The five manufacturers were Leonard F. Porter, Inc., J. L. Houston Manufacturing Co., Oceanic Trading Co., and Northwest Arts in Seattle; and Western Novelty Co. in Portland. The wholesaler was Indian Arts and Crafts in Seattle. The news release stated that:

> According to complaints, the firms market imitations of carved and etched merchandise traditionally made by Alaskan Native Americans. These items are made wholly or partly of authentic or simulated ivory, baleen or soapstone, materials which are used by Native Alaskan craftspersons. In some instances, the merchandise is signed with Alaskan Native American-type names such as "Apodruk" [they were in error here: this is Harry Apodruk, employed by Porter], "Nuguruk" and "Nunuk." No disclosure is made that the merchandise is made outside of Alaska, or that machinery is used in carving and/or etching it.
>
> The complaints allege that the appearance of the products, combined with the materials, labels and signatures used, mislead the public to believe the merchandise has been hand-made by Alaskan Native Americans in Alaska.
>
> [The proposed orders would]: Require the attachment of labels which would clearly disclose the origin of such items and the use of machinery in their production.
>
> Prohibit the signing of Alaskan Native American-type names to the merchandise unless it is hand-made by a Native Alaskan.
>
> Require respondents to obtain a signed statement from re-sellers agreeing to conform with the order, and to stop making sales to those who do not agree to be bound by it.
>
> The respondents have been given the opportunity to advise the FTC whether they are interested in having the proceedings disposed of by the entry of consent orders.

On 21 June 1974, with the consent order negotiations unsuccessful, complaints were issued to the six companies for a hearing to be adjudicated by a Federal Trade Commission judge in administrative law. The hearing was scheduled for Seattle in September 1975, and I was asked to be a witness for the Federal Trade Commission. As a fairly well-known advocate of Alaskan art, I knew that I was expected to give testimony for the prosecution, yet I was somewhat reluctant to oppose the one company, Leonard F. Porter, Inc., which had employed so many Alaskan Eskimo artists. It seemed to me that Porter's company did not quite fit in the complaint. But I also knew that testimony could go both ways, and indeed it did. The lawyers for the companies were well prepared and the judge was well relaxed in his easy chair during the one day I was present at the hearing, so I was not surprised when the *Seattle Post-Intelligencer* (4 March 1976) reported in big headlines: "Judge Throws Out Charges on Curios." The decision, said the newspaper, was that the purchasers of the items were not misled; one of the FTC charges was described as "bordering on the outlandish" and another as "not warranting serious discussion."

I doubt if 90 percent of purchasers can distinguish the Alaskan Native objects from those made elsewhere. Because the artist is part of an object's value (the collector of Picasso's doesn't want copies!), plans were already afoot in Alaska to combat the invasion of fraudulent goods before the Federal Trade Commission hearing. Consequently, in 1971 the Alaska Division of Economic Enterprise developed the "Silver Hand" emblem, which is attached to "authentic" Alaskan articles. This has not been greeted with 100 percent joy by the gift shops in Alaska. To some, this discriminates against art produced by non-Natives who are not working with Eskimo or Indian themes, and silently implies that, because of its being singled out, the "Silver Hand" product is superior. This tag has probably proved helpful to many customers who would otherwise have had to ask an uninformed clerk. But, in the long run, it is the responsibility of the merchant to provide information for the customer, who can then decide whether to choose something made in Seattle or Alaska.

Reproductions and Deceptions

Many a time I have seen painters at work, making copies of great paintings in museums, but nowadays there are photographic and mechanical means of obtaining exact copies. Almost all of these are recognized for what they are—copies, but some have been falsely sold as originals. The same path was followed when the collecting of Eskimo artifacts became popular—reproductions, copies, and outright fakes came to the market. I had my first lesson in deceptive practices when I served coffee in our little restaurant in Nome one day in 1946. Every summer Nome was invaded by itinerant salespeople, many of whom targeted the Eskimos who wandered up and down Front Street. One of these peddlers was a man whose principal merchandise was eyeglasses, but who had other mysterious sidelines, one of which was selling "old" artifacts. As he drank his coffee, trying to counteract the effects of his latest hangover, he confided that he was on his way to Fort Davis (six miles east of Nome) to dig up some wooden tools that an Eskimo man had made for him a few weeks before. "I've got a live one," he said, meaning a tourist at the hotel. When he came for coffee the next day he was very happy. "Those tools looked real old," he said.

Another deceptive practice has been the coloring of new ivory with various substances to make it look old, since old ivory has always been considered to be more valuable than new ivory. I had not seen any dyed ivory until I bought a chunky bracelet colored green and black—just to have an artificially dyed piece for my collection—from Mack's Totem Curio Shop near the Seattle waterfront in 1956. Mr. Albert ("Mack") McKillop, the proprietor, gave me valuable pointers on how to distinguish the genuine from the false, one of which is the sharper definition of the grain of the naturally colored ivory, especially in the core section.

Museums throughout the world sell reproductions of the ethnic art in their holdings, and many an Egyptian or pre-Columbian artifact hangs from a human neck! The most popular Eskimo objects are cribbage boards, figurines, and masks, usually made of materials that cannot be confused with those characteristic of the originals. Nowadays in Alaska, however, there are many mask makers, both Native and non-Native, who make copies of old masks. Under certain circumstances, these copies could be misidentified as originals. In 1976 I saw a copy of an old Point Hope mask hanging on the wall of a new Native-owned shop in Anchorage. The original was purchased in 1939 by Helge Larsen and Froelich Rainey from an old woman named Nashugrak, who had found it among a cache of fifty masks under an old dance-house floor (Rainey 1959:11, 12). I knew that the original was safely housed in the Danish National Museum in Copenhagen, but this copy was a dandy. As a friend and I waited to inquire about the mask, we could not help overhearing what the clerk (the owner?) was discussing with a woman who wanted to buy a mask, but not the one on the wall, because it did not "look like an Eskimo mask." She asked what others they had for sale, and the man replied that they had none in stock, "but that's no problem," and he reached under the counter and pulled out my book on Eskimo masks. "We can make any mask you want from this book," he said.

The newest material used to form the shapes of walrus tusks and sperm whale teeth for scrimshaw work is polymer plastic. Some of these "false teeth," "bogus scrimshaw," or "forgeries," as they are variously called, have mold marks identifying them as reproductions by the companies who produce them, but some do not. A mold mark does not guarantee that a piece will always be considered a reproduction, because mold marks can be deliberately obliterated by unscrupulous sellers. Most of the polymer pieces in the market today are copies of whalers' scrimshaw—taken from originals, or with invented scenes and ships in the old style. It has been said that people have been fooled by these pieces, but the ones I have seen definitely had the appearance of copies made of a manufactured substance.

Scrimshaw Copies on Plastic (figure 73)

Plastic sperm whale teeth are excellent examples of scrimshaw copies which I would not mistake for real ivory; yet, to someone who has never seen real sperm whale teeth, they might indeed be thought genuine. Figure 73, the *Thrasher* tooth is made in a mold to catch the engraving and is then colored black. The plastic itself has been dyed various shades of tan to look old. Each lengthwise face of the tooth depicts a ship in Arctic seas: one side pictures men in a boat and on the ice in an area of frosty hills; the other scene is with walrus on ice floes. STEAMER THRASHER is engraved in capital letters above one of the ships. The inner curve of the tooth, separating the two ships from below, is engraved with a single phrase: WHALING IN THE ARCTIC. The outer curve is ornamented with two whaling harpoons, crossed.[2]

Another reproduction in plastic is a so-called hunting score from Point Barrow, made by LaValle Studios of Portland, Oregon (fig. 73). Except for size, this is reproduced exactly from an illustration in Hoffman's "Graphic Art of the Eskimo" (1897: fig. 99). The original is 4.8 inches long; the reproduction, not quite 4 inches. According to the description, copied by Hoffman from John Murdoch's *Point Barrow Eskimo,* the original of this piece was colored red, but this copy is black. The reproduction is sold in an envelope with "archaeological replica" printed in large letters. A brief note (also with "archaeological replica" printed in red letters) quotes Murdoch's explanation of the engraved figures which, briefly, is that a young hunter and his son killed six "reindeer" (it should read "caribou" for Murdoch's time), one on land, but the rest speared in the water from a kayak (1897:877).

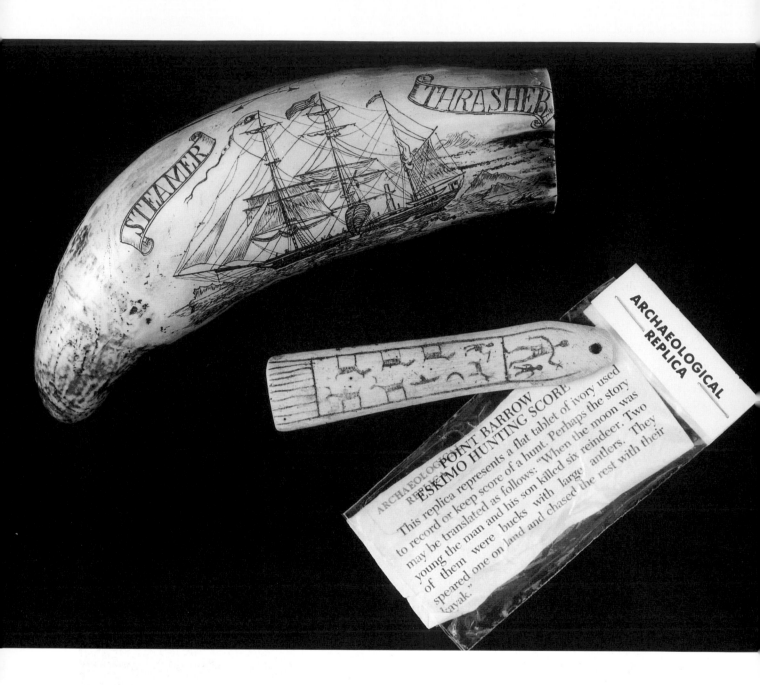

Fig. 73. Polymer plastic replicas. A: Steam whaler *Thrasher*, in shape of sperm whale tooth. 1992. 6¼"; B: Point Barrow hunting score. 1990. Almost 4"

Recent Scrimshaw on Old Ivory (figure 74)

The molded plastic articles as represented by the sperm whale tooth and the hunting score (fig. 73) will probably never be considered originals, but objects similar to two pieces in this collection (fig. 74), which are engravings of the 1980s made on prehistoric ivory, have already entered the market as ancient pictographs at high prices. These pieces were engraved by non-Native scrimshanders from nineteenth-century pictures copied from books. Since they are engraved on prehistoric tools and slat armor, the uninitiated buyer thinks that the engraving dates back 500 to 1,500 years.

I first became aware of this work when I received a photograph for identification of two pieces of bone slat armor engraved with pictographs that were familiar to me (see illus. 18). The bottom piece in the photograph had three scenes copied from Hoffman's book: one was a dance scene from a drill bow attributed to Kotzebue Sound; another, two men from a Sledge Island drill bow; the third, a figure with arms upraised from an unidentified "shaman's drum" (Hoffman 1897:915, 923).[3]

I subsequently received many more inquiries, some from people who had parted with a substantial amount of money. Even dealers get fooled by these pieces, one of which (shown in illus. 19), mounted on a lucite display stand, sold for $1,500. The original price was not more than $60. The pictographs on this piece were also copied from Hoffman's illustrations: men making a bow, a man mending a net, and dancers (Hoffman 1897:852, 868, 870). The woman who bought this object was reimbursed by the dealer.

Sotheby's has advertised similar pieces twice in their American Indian Art sales catalogs, but none was sold, or else they were withdrawn (Seven pieces in lot 364, sale 5785, 29 November 1988, suggested price, $2,000–$3,000; and five pieces in lot 309, sale 6245, 26 November 1991, suggested price, $2,500–$3,500. If sold at their

Illus. 18. Two pieces of bone slat armor, several hundred years old, on which pictographs from nineteenth-century drill bows have recently been engraved. Figures from Hoffman 1897. Top: making a bow, p. 868; mending a net, p. 852; dancing, p. 870. Bottom: dancing, Kotzebue Sound, p. 915; man with bird, Sledge Island, p. 923. Photograph courtesy of Field Museum of Natural History, Chicago, neg. no. A-110389

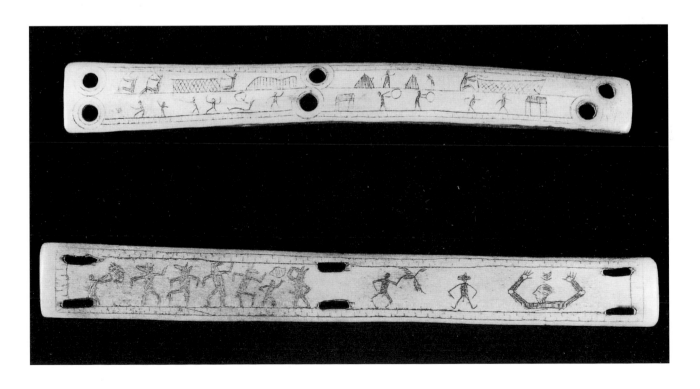

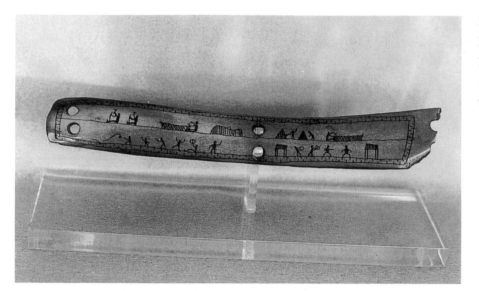

Illus. 19. Graphic designs from Hoffman's "Graphic Art of the Eskimo" (1897), engraved in the 1980s on ancient slat armor dug up on St. Lawrence Island

original cost from non-Native scrimshanders, lot 364 would have been priced at $280–$350, and lot 309, at $200–$250.) Two items in sale 6245 had exactly the same designs as the pieces in illustration 18.

The two objects in the present collection (fig. 74) were purchased in Port Townsend in the early 1990s. Both are old ivory with lovely brown and tan patination. The larger piece is probably part of a broken harpoon counterweight. It is engraved with caribou, two whales, a man with a fishing net, people in a boat, a walrus, men fighting with bows and arrows, some geometric designs, and the ubiquitous dance scene from a Kotzebue Sound drill bow.

The smaller piece, of original undetermined use and with two holes drilled through, has a fishing net scene, six caribou (one of which has just been shot with an arrow), and a man chasing a flock of birds. The edges of both artifacts are engraved with the alternating spur design that was so popular on eighteenth- and nineteenth-century objects. A tag attached to the smaller piece declared it to be a "fossil walrus ivory" Eskimo artifact pictograph, 500 years old, from St. Lawrence Island, Alaska. There was no notice that the pictographs were engraved within the past few years.

The use of old ivory as a base for new engravings by both Natives and non-Natives is fairly common. St. Lawrence Island is a prime source, as are sites along the coast in Northwest Alaska. Many of the objects are taken from private or tribal lands, but some are taken illegally from federal lands. In 1993 the National Park Service, concerned about the looting from federally owned lands, drafted two

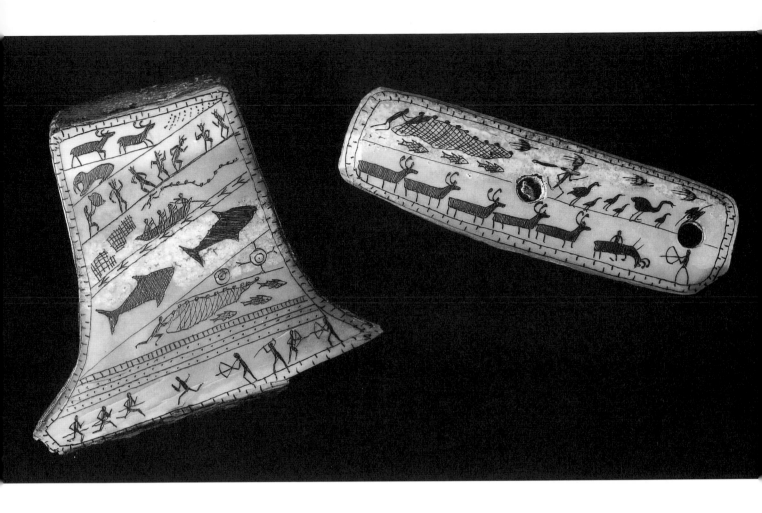

Fig. 74. Anonymous. Old ivory fragments with recent engravings. A: Nineteenth-century pictographs engraved in 1992 on old brown ivory from St. Lawrence Island sites. (The dancing scene is copied from Hoffman 1897:915.) 2⅝"; B: Nineteenth-century pictographs engraved on 500-year-old ivory from St. Lawrence Island sites. 1990s. 3½"

versions of a brochure to be issued to the public on archeological resource protection, outlining already existing laws, and issuing a warning against further looting. Native artisans, after reviewing the drafts, felt that the brochure would have a negative impact on the sale of their art, much of which is done on old ivory that, according to them, is taken from their tribal lands. This is not a concern of the Park Service, but the Alaskan artists worry that emphasis on the prohibition of digging on federal lands may lead the public to believe erroneously that all of their work on old pieces is from illegally obtained material, when most of it actually comes from the private lands like St. Lawrence Island. The sale of artifacts from mining the St. Lawrence sites is said to bring much-needed cash to the Eskimos (a recent "winged object" brought $5,750 at a Sotheby's sale in 1993, and an Okvik doll sold for $29,900 at a Christie's auction in 1994), but it is also said that so much damage has been done on the sites that many are now worthless for scientific study.[4]

Plaster Copy of a Soapstone Carving (figure 75)

I do not remember the exact date I bought this copy of an Inuit carving of a woman with a baby, but it was sometime in the early 1970s. I do not know the source of the piece, either, but it probably came from the Toronto company that, according to a *Seattle Times* article (12 August 1972), was producing a thousand units of eighteen different animal and human figures every day. This piece is made of plaster painted black, and by no stretch of the imagination would it be mistaken for an original stone carving. For someone who had longed for an original stone carving at the then-price of $200–300, one of these figurines, with the highest price of $5.98, would have been a satisfactory solution.

As with totem poles made in Taiwan and ivory figurines in Seattle, the Inuit copies have come in for their share of criticism. But oddly, the criticism stems mainly from the appropriation of a design that supposedly "belongs" to the Inuit artists. This kind of criticism is also prevalent in Alaska against non-Natives and Natives alike who borrow ideas not their own. An extreme example has to do with the Inuit sculpture, the style of which was copied by Alaskan Eskimos a few years after it became popular. No doubt the Canadian carvers and distributors did not like the competition and copycat production, although the output was only a fraction of the Canadians', but the harshest criticism came from potential buyers in Alaska. About twenty years ago a Bureau of Indian Affairs official told us that he was "furious" that his wife had bought a soapstone carving that Robert Mayokok was selling. He said that Alaskan Eskimos should not be doing that kind of work, which rightly "belonged" to the Canadian Eskimos.

The appropriation of themes, styles, and form in art has been going on from time immemorial all over the world. After the arrival of Europeans in Alaska, the first appropriators were the Eskimos themselves who used western designs and subjects in their engravings and adapted shapes of foreign origin in their basketry and wood and ivory objects. Today it is a two-way street: Native artists of the 1990s borrow themes from past cultures, and some, like the late Jim Schoppert, a Tlingit artist, borrow from other tribal groups. Schoppert copied photographs of Eskimo portraits for his greeting cards, and just before his death (in 1992), he carved a series of masks like those collected on Kodiak Island in 1842. Many non-Native artists in Alaska have used Eskimo themes. One of the most interesting of these (apparently inspired by the *Inua* publication in

Fig. 75. Anonymous, Canadian Inuit. Female figurine. Plaster-of-paris imitating soapstone. 1980s. 4½"

1982) is a poster, "Inua Spirit," by Jon Van Zyle, in which a half-man half-dog face, with a fur ruff and two hands with holes, is surrounded by circles, as in the old Eskimo masks.[5]

The Billiken

A collection of Alaskan artifacts is not complete without a few billikens. This object, which appears to have been modeled after a Buddha, was invented by Florence Pretz, an art teacher in Kansas City, Missouri, but it became by adoption one of the most famous—if not infamous—Alaskan ivory carvings of all time. Its fame rests not only on its huge production (in the thousands, and probably in the millions) after it was first copied by Alaskan carvers in ivory about 1909 but also on the popular good-luck attributes applied to it by its inventor and the original manufacturer, the Billiken Company of Chicago, which were expanded upon by the merchants of Nome.

The billiken had two peaks of popularity in Alaska: first, during its initial production of the early 1910s; and again, during World War II when the flyers at Marks Airfield adjacent to Nome accepted it as a good-luck pocket piece. By the 1990s its popularity was waning, and I predict that it will be only a collector's curio in the future. When I first lived in Nome I tried to learn about the billiken's origin, but the 1940s apparently were too far away from the billiken fad following Miss Pretz's patent for an "ornamental image" on 6 October 1908. I learned about the patent from the number (39,603) on the back of an iron bank that I purchased later in Seattle. That number applied only to the billiken figure, and another number (indecipherable) was for the throne on which the billiken sat.

The Billiken Company, which had acquired the manufacturing rights, immediately produced the figurine in amazing variety: statuettes, incense burners, pillow covers, glass jars, puzzles, postcards, soft-bodied dolls, belt buckles, the coin bank—even as marshmallows, someone told me! It was featured in songs, and various slogans featuring the good-luck theme were made up for the figurines and postcards.

I learned about the billiken's Alaskan origin when Michael Kazingnuk told me in 1955 that someone had brought one of the originals to Nome about 1909 or 1910 for Happy Jack, his brother-in-law, to copy in ivory. Although it might have been one of the original Chicago-made billikens, I suspect that it was one of the plaster-of-paris billikens that was adopted as the "patron saint" for the Alaska-Yukon Pacific Exposition in Seattle in 1909. Whatever the source, it immediately became a hot item for the inhabitants of Nome, who at that time seemed partial to tasteless curios (the fine engraving excepted!). Despite its appearance as a caricature of an Eskimo—and many people have mistakenly believed that it was an aboriginal sculpture—the billiken has been a staple of many a carver's production, especially for carvers who are not especially talented. In the early days when walrus ivory was plentiful they were made as large as a tusk permitted, but also, in extremely small size, a sought-after collector's item.

Throughout the succeeding decades in Alaska, although new slogans were invented and the figures were changed in various details, they were always recognizable as billikens. The billiken also had further travels: as the mascot for the St. Louis University athletic teams; as an item of Siberian Chukchi folklore; and, in 1911, as the symbol and mascot for the Royal Order of Jesters, a philanthropic segment of the Shriners. In recent times it has been manufactured as pottery cups, salt shakers, candles, vases, and as silver good luck charms for bracelets. It has been used in the names of magazines, cocktail lounges, children's clubs, ski clubs, theaters, and shoes. It has been put to many other uses, as well, and indeed the height of its fame, literally, was attained by a wooden billiken perched atop a Tlingit-style totem pole, as reported in the *Alaska Sportsman* (April 1959) and as illustrated on the cover of a pamphlet, *Indians, Eskimos and Aleuts of Alaska,* published in 1968 by the Bureau of Indian Affairs, U.S. Department of the Interior. (The back cover has an illustration of a seal carved of walnut by Peter Seeganna.)

I have written about the billiken in two articles as well as in my books, with enough details to satisfy any collector of minutiae, and although the billiken may be lacking in artistic qualities, it has provided an income for many an impoverished carver, bringing fun and maybe even a bit of good luck to those who possess one (Ray 1960; 1961:122–24; 1974; 1977:45).

The billikens (figs. 76–79) in this collection represent a sampling of objects made throughout the years, from the original ones to those popular today. The plaster-of-paris billiken (fig. 76), 4½ inches high, sits unattached on a throne 6½ inches high. A medallion embedded in the bottom of the billiken reads: "Billiken trade mark. Copyright 1908 by The Craftsman's Guild. Pat. Oct. 6, 1908. The Billiken Company, Chicago. The God of Things as they Ought to be." A medallion on the back of the throne reads: "Billiken Throne. Copyright 1908 by The Billiken Company, Chicago, 1908. Billiken,

The God of Things as they Ought to be." The original metal banks were the same size as this object, but instead of "The God of Things as they Ought to be," only the words "Billiken, Good Luck" were sometimes written on the throne.

Figures 77A and D are examples of the many commercial variations on the billiken. Figure 77A was made as a mascot for the Jesters, as mentioned earlier. On the base of this billiken is the slogan "Mirth is King." The initials "ROJ" (Royal Order of Jesters) are attached to the feet. The Jesters also used the billiken motif on

Fig. 76. Chicago-made Billiken. Plaster-of-paris. 1908. Height of throne 6½"; height of billiken 4½"

Fig. 77. Chicago-made Billikens. A: Metal. Made for the Royal Order of Jesters. Probably 1970s; B: Framed postcard. 1908; C: Glass bottle with metal cap. 1908. 4″ tall; D: Candle. Probably 1970s. 4½″

drinking glasses and on jewelry such as pendants, tie clasps, cuff links, and key chains.[6] The framed postcard (fig. 77B) is colored in tan, green, and gold. Beneath the picture is the verse: "My coming drives the blues away—'Twill prove a bright red letter day—Billiken." The glass bottle billiken (fig. 77C) is capped by a metal screw hat and also has the usual long slogan around the base: "The God of Things . . . " The candle (fig. 77D) was made by Candles of Nome, probably in the 1970s, and was called a "billikin" candle, a misspelling often used for the patented billiken name.

The three Eskimo-made figurines in the collection (figs. 78, 79) are 3 to 3½ inches high, which is also rather larger than most. The billiken in figure 78A was made in the 1920s from walrus ivory. The billiken in figure 78B, carved of sperm whale tooth, was made at a much later date and was darkened with dye at the Porter establishment in Seattle. It is signed on the bottom: "Thomas Ekak,

Fig. 78. A: Anonymous, probably Nome. Billiken. Walrus ivory. 1920s. 3½"; B: Thomas Ekak, Wainwright. Billiken. Sperm whale tooth, artificially dyed. Made for Leonard F. Porter, Inc., Seattle. 1959. 3½"

Fig. 79. Ben Saclamana, King Island. Billiken. Soapstone. About 1972. 3"

Wainwright, Alaska, May 6, 1959." The soapstone billiken (fig. 79), which I purchased in Seattle in 1972, was made by Ben Saclamana of King Island.

It is perhaps inappropriate to end this book with a discussion of the billiken, the least indigenous and artistic of the Alaskan ivory carvings and the least liked by the carvers, but it characterizes the flexibility of the twentieth-century ivory artisans and their willingness to adapt new ideas. These traits probably were rooted in prehistoric times, for there is evidence of borrowing and adaptation in the Okvik and Old Bering Sea cultures of 1,500–2,000 years ago; in Eskimo coiled basketry; and probably in the pictorial engraving on ivory that culminated in the unusual drill bows; and in the later works by Happy Jack.

Culture exchange gives vigor and breadth to art at all times and in all places. It has given strength to Alaskan art in many ways and dimensions. The ideas that today's younger generation utilize from their studies in seminars, universities, and schools devoted to general Native American arts have given their works a challenging vitality; and the use of Native themes by non-Natives has brought a wealth of recognition to a remarkable people. It becomes a murky field only when things are called something they are not; when the intangible part that is "artist" is taken away through fraud.

Appendix
Lily Ekak Savok's Picture Writing

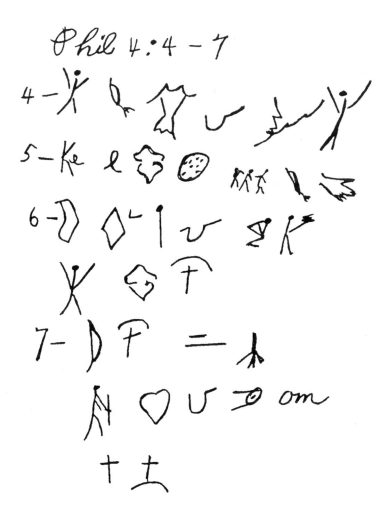

Philippians 4:47, as written in picture writing by Lily Ekok Savok in 1968. The symbols are traced from her pencil drawing, and the Eskimo translation is transcribed from her handwritten copy. This illustration is not part of the University of Alaska Museum

collection, but it is integral to the discussion of picture writing, especially since it was information given directly to me by one of the inventors of the system; and Philippians 4:47 was her favorite verse.

4. *Koviasogin sungeroadkon utermaik: solee niplit-kik-soonga Koviasogin.*
Rejoice (the man "is happy") **in the Lord** (biceps) **always** (dress "because the word *dress* sounds like it in Eskimo") **and** (a "dipper of soup sounds like *and*") **again I say** (mouth or face, "*nipluqsuq,* or make a sound") **rejoice.**

5. *Kee keeniknukteeroong agangilin elokinon enung-noon. Uton sungeeroak etook ar-ga-ngnee.*
Let your moderation ("symbols to remember *keeniknukteeroong*") **be known** (sealskin. "A white pretty sealskin in winter, *naleq,* is similar to *nalungichiga,* to know") **unto all** (dots enclosed by circle mean "lots of things together" or all) **men** (several men) **the Lord is at hand** (drawing of a hand).

6. *Isumalo-yang i gion: ksimi sopayak Aga u likon solee pika-golikoon topiklogo koyan-mik kee peegeesookan eleecho-git-kaa-goong.*
Be careful ("just a symbol") **for nothing** ("a diamond is precious; check means take away and there is nothing") **but in everything by prayer** (prayer sounds almost like pencil in Eskimo) **and supplication** (man kneeling) **with thanksgiving** (man holds goods for which he is thankful) **let your requests** (man beseeching from heaven) **be made known** (sealskin) **unto God** (God is cross beneath rainbow).

7. *Ovalee keenwenum Agertum kangeemateroam elooknin kungiksitmin, kownageseega Omatim solee esoomatin omoona Christ Jesus.*
And the peace (dipper is not used, for Eskimo translation is *ovalee,* meaning "so that" instead of and. "The words bow (*keluinuq*) and peace (*kiuniuq*) sound almost alike in Eskimo") **of God which passeth** ("the bottom line passes the top line") **all understanding** (symbol for understanding is roots of a tree) **shall keep** (shepherd with staff "keeping his flock") **your hearts** (Mrs. Savok had memorized this word as singular and therefore used only one heart) **and minds** ("in Eskimo, end of a log also means mind") **through** ("om is a reminder for *omoona*") **Christ** (a cross) **Jesus** (cross placed into the earth).

Notes

How It Started and Where It Went

1. Himmelheber collected some objects from the Nome area, and in the second German edition he illustrated "Zwei Gesichter an einer Grabstele (Kuskokwimstrom)," in fig. 25. These masks are not from Kuskokwim River graves, but are the "good and bad shaman" masks made by the King Islanders. There is another mistaken mask in fig. 9 of the second German edition and in fig. 39 in the English edition. Himmelheber says that it is from Anvik, but *The Far North* catalog ascribes it to the lower Kuskokwim River, with the date September 1881. The mask is in the Hamburgisches Museum für Völkerkunde und Vorgeschichte (National Gallery of Art, 1973, fig. 161).

2. I had already examined rather superficially, but not photographed, the collections in the Alaska State Museum, the University of Alaska Museum, and the Washington State Museum (University of Washington). Later I also examined the collections of several other museums, including the Sheldon Jackson Museum in Sitka, Alaska.

3. In 1962, however, I had given a paper, "The Eskimo and the Land: Ownership and Utilization," at the Thirteenth Alaskan Science Conference. It was published in the proceedings of the conference but was so shortened in the editing that it is almost meaningless.

4. Thora Katchatag's photograph appears five times as an unidentified person in Evelyn Stefansson's *Here Is Alaska* (1943). There are many other photographs of Alaskan scenes and Eskimo people, especially from Unalakleet, but few are identified. Frederick Machetanz took the photos of Unalakleet, but he identified only two white men by name: Emil Fisher, a schoolteacher, and Charles A. Traeger, his uncle. I took a copy of the book, which is included in this artifact collection, to Unalakleet in 1968, and Martha Nanouk identified the photos for me. I have added the identifications to the captions. One of the photographs, a child cupping the face of a woman (Thora), ready to give her a kiss, appears to

be the model for a card, "An Eskimo Kiss," issued by the Alaska Crippled Children's organization in the 1960s.

5. Papers in *Ethnohistory in the Arctic* (Ray 1983) include translation and information about the Vasil'ev-Shishmarev expedition to the Arctic, 1819–22; early maritime trade with the Bering Strait Eskimos; "The Kheuveren Legend"; St. Michael in the nineteenth century; historical signal posts in Kotzebue Sound; the Omilak silver mine; detailed information about Charlie and Mary Antisarlook's reindeer herd; picture writing; Eskimo place-names in Bering Strait; and the two polity and settlement pattern papers already mentioned. The place-name paper, which appeared earlier in the journal *Names* (1971b), was the first to map and relate the names to tribal occupancy.

6. The Robert H. Lowie Museum of Anthropology has been renamed the Phoebe Apperson Hearst Museum of Anthropology.

7. In Dockstader's book, figure 78, "Parka and Boots," is misattributed to the "Bering Straits [*sic*], Alaska." It is, instead, from northern Canada.

8. In the 1950s, however, the Indian Arts and Crafts Board was beginning to give financial aid to promising young Indian artists, one of whom, Ronald Senungetuk, a graduate of Mt. Edgecumbe boarding school in Sitka, was awarded a scholarship by the Board in cooperation with the D.A.R. National Indians' Committee and the D.A.R. States Indians' Committees (*Smoke Signals*, 1953). Senungetuk, an Inupiaq from Wales, later received a Fulbright grant and studied art in Denmark. He became the first teacher in the Native Art program at the University of Alaska Fairbanks in 1965.

Howard Rock, whose work is discussed on pages 149–51, was the first Eskimo to study art in college—without grants and scholarships—but he did not graduate. He studied in both the art and anthropology departments, especially with Verne F. Ray.

Contemporary Graphics

1. Robert Mayokok also published several articles in the *Alaska Sportsman*, but these articles, such as "My Life as an Eskimo" (August and September 1955), have been heavily edited (perhaps rewritten?), which lessens the charm of his own phraseology.

2. The correct name is Alaska Treasure Shop (not Treasure Shop, as reported in various publications).

3. When he was in Seattle, Bernard wrote me an interesting note about the meaning of *Ukiuvuk,* the name of King Island. He said that he had "met Sergei [Bogojavlensky, who had done research on King Island] and we've been friends for few months while he was up in Nome. I had lots of fun listening to him trying Ukiuvokmiu dialect. He may be right OOGEE OOK ugiuk is winter ugiukpuk—big winter, may mean big time of winter in that part. Actually to us it's just a name for the island UKIUVUK" (Katexac to author, 30 March 1970).

4. The Helper Neck Bible is uncataloged in the Helper Neck Collection, MS 574, Archives, Alaska and Polar Regions Department, Elmer E. Rasmuson Library, University of Alaska Fairbanks.

5. I do not know the correct spelling of Amigitchoak. Sarah's sister, Alice, was

a teacher, and their surname was spelled variously Omigetjoak, Omekitjook, and Omekejook in the yearly education reports. Covenant Church records in Unalakleet spell it Omekitjoak, and L. Arden Almquist in his book, *Covenant Missions in Alaska*, spells it both Omegichuak and Omegitjoak (Almquist 1962: 49, 52). Almquist wrote that Jacob Kenick had taught first at Koyuk, and then had spent thirty-five years as a missionary at Hooper Bay, Shaktoolik, and Nunivak Island, where, "with their conversion, the Island people (including the medicine woman) all left their idols, throwing them into the sea" (ibid.:52).

Mainly Women's Work

1. In my article, "Bering Strait Eskimo" (Ray 1984d), a caption to an illustration of two baskets reads that the similarity between the two "may be due to the Moravian missionaries who worked in both areas [i.e., Alaska and Labrador]" (1984d: 298). This assumes that the Moravians were the originators of the coiling basketry technique in Alaska, but they were not. I did not write that caption (nor any of the others in that article), and I am not responsible for its erroneous assumption.

2. Margaret Johnsson told me that the word *kuspuk* originated, as far as she knew, in the 1940s in the Yukon River area, and then it traveled north to Unalakleet, which is on the border of Yup'ik and Inupiaq speech. The word *kuspuk* was adopted by writers, but northern Eskimos call it a *cloth parka*. The word *parka* is not an original Native Alaskan word. The word *parky* was borrowed by the early Russians from the Siberian Kamchadal language, and this is still the pronunciation used in Alaska.

3. Information about the Nome Skin Sewers Cooperative Association is from my field notes.

Wood

1. Instead of "vivid scenes" in English translation, the original German phrase, *lebhafteren Szenen,* would be better translated here as "lively" or "sprightly" (Himmelheber 1993: 23; 1953: 37).

2. A comprehensive survey of Yup'ik painting is found in Ray 1981: 39–44.

3. The Alaska State Museum in Juneau has a good example of a whaling bucket with carved ivory animals in the handle and on the sides but without the requisite ivory chains, which Kazingnuk said were absolutely necessary, at least in the Bering Strait region. This bucket supposedly came from Point Barrow and was sold in the 1910s to Daniel S. Neuman, a Nome-based physician who was an ardent collector of artifacts, many of which he sold to the Territory of Alaska, which led, in turn, to the founding of the museum. The bucket became available for purchase from Neuman's granddaughter in 1986, but since the museum was short of funds, the Friends of the Alaska State Museum and Chevron U.S.A. purchased it and donated it to the museum (Newsletter, Division of State Museums, Fall 1986).

4. By the 1970s I had collected a great deal of information and many

photographs of this unique mortuary art, which I included in *Aleut and Eskimo Art,* but expanded for an article in *American Indian Art* in 1982. The seventeen illustrations range from Nelson's drawing of monuments that he saw at Tununak in 1878, to photographs taken by schoolteacher Clark Garber in 1930.

5. I know of only four folktales in which an owl is a prominent character, although there probably are more. Margaret Lantis obtained one from Nunivak Island and Edwin S. Hall, Jr., recorded four from Noatak. In the tale, "The Owl," from Nunivak, an owl and his family had trouble with a "joking friend." Two of the Noatak tales feature an owl as a shaman: "The mountain called Aiyassiruk" (I think that this is Ayasayuk, the old village at Cape Nome), and "The Ungaluklik [Unalakleet] and Suttulik [Shaktoolik] People Fight." In another tale, "The girl who married an owl," a stubborn girl married a stranger who was an owl in disguise (Lantis 1946:300; Hall 1975:282–84, 396–97, 399).

Pictorial Engraving or Eskimo Scrimshaw

1. Nelson did not collect objects from Kauwerak; Jacobsen, however, obtained several drill bows from there which are illustrated in *Amerika's Nordwest-Küste. . .* , 1884, pl. 9, no. 16, and pl. 10, nos. 7 and 13. There are also five drill bows in the Etholén collection in the National Museum of Finland, said to have come from "Kauwerak Bay" and Norton Sound, and given to the museum by Adolf Etholén in 1846. It is not known "which bow is which," but all are similar to those collected by both Jacobsen and Nelson. Etholén apparently obtained the drill bows in trade, because he did not visit either Norton Sound or the village of Kauwerak. (See Varjola 1990:279–83 for photographs and line drawings.)

2. This estimate of Eskimo deaths is probably close to the actual number. Many who died were buried in a common trench grave. A notebook in the Nome Methodist Church contains a list of 173 Eskimos who died between 1 November 1918, and January 1919, a remarkable number since many Eskimos were not known by name. Included in the list are the names of Happy Jack and "Mrs. Happy Jack"("Lavinia Wallace Young Mission" notebook, pages 13–33).

3. Apparently all of the Wales school children were avid artists who produced pencil and crayon drawings of reindeer herding, camp life, dancing, fishing, and drumming—as well as "foreign" subjects like houses and the revenue cutter *Bear.* Only a few names such as Adlooat, Ootenna (George Ootenna), and Nexatite have come down to us, mainly because their illustrations were used in the *Eskimo Bulletin,* a yearly "newspaper" printed at Wales, or were preserved by the teachers. A collection of anonymous pencil and crayon drawings was kept by the Lopps, and another collection of drawings by Ootenna is now in the Peary Macmillan Arctic Museum at Bowdoin College in Brunswick, Maine (Kathleen Lopp Smith to author, Seattle, 28 April 1993; Susan Kaplan to author, Bowdoin College, 30 September 1993).

4. Biographical information about Komonaseak is from his daughter, Frieda Larsen, and Caroline M. Reader, both of Nome. I am indebted to Kathleen Lopp Smith for obtaining Komonaseak's photograph for me.

Canadian Inuit Art

1. A footnote to this early collecting should be made here. George Swinton wrote that "some credit be given to the late Dr. Jacques Rousseau of the Centre d'Etudes nordiques at Laval University [because] during 1947 and 1948 he did field work in Ungava and started to collect 'Eskimo art' not as souvenirs but as an art form. In the summer of 1948 he met James Houston in Povungnituk and showed him carvings which Qupirqualuk had casually carved. . . . Some of these pieces were shown at that famous first sale at the Guild in Montreal; and later, through Houston's writing, Qupirqualuk became one of the very first individual artists to be known" (Swinton 1972:126).

2. One of the stray copies of the manual is in this collection.

3. One of the most recent booklets, *Canadian Inuit Sculpture,* was issued by the Indian and Northern Affairs Canada in 1992. Thirty-five objects of bone, ivory, and stone from twenty-five villages are illustrated with complete documentation in this nineteen-page booklet, which is distributed free of charge. One page is also devoted to an explanation of "materials and methods"; a two-page map locates all producing villages; and the Eskimo syllabic writing system is explained.

Athabascan Chief's Coat

1. For a survey of beaded designs see *Northern Athapaskan Art* (1989) by Kate C. Duncan.

Can This Be Eskimo Art?

1. The use of only one name on an object apparently was to make it seem authentically "Eskimo"—but all Eskimo artists in Alaska at that time used the binomial; for example, George Ahgupuk, Robert Mayokok, Kivetoruk Moses, and Wilbur Walluk.

2. In 1984 John Bockstoce sent me a list of the "bogus scrimshaw" that was known at that time: whale teeth, walrus tusks, panbone, and other whalers' scrimshaw.

3. Hoffman did not provide provenience for the dancing figures or the two Sledge Island men, but I have identified them from drill bows in the Smithsonian Institution: Kotzebue Sound drill bow, number 48522, and Sledge Island drill bow, number 45025. I have been unable to find the original of the "shaman's drum."

4. In another Sotheby's sale, a human figurine sold for $7,000, but an Okvik head, 3⅜ inches high, with a suggested price of $25,000–$35,000, either did not sell or was withdrawn (Sale 5785, 29 November 1988, lots 190 and 193).

5. *Inua: Spirit World of the Bering Sea Eskimo,* Fitzhugh and Kaplan, editors. The title of this publication should have been *Yua,* or else *Inua and Yua,* because the word, *inua,* meaning "its person" (of an object or an animal) is derived from Inupiaq, the northern Eskimo language, but most of the objects illustrated and

discussed in the book, *Inua,* are from the Yup'ik area, where the term for "person" is *yua.* For example, the *inua* of the salmon portrayed in the mask, figure 71, should read *yua* of the salmon, because it came from "south of the lower Yukon."

6. In 1968 I received a copy of "The Origin of the Billiken," which is a summary of one man's search for the origin of the billiken symbol used by the Jesters. Carnie A. Generaux, a member of the Los Angeles Court Royal Order of Jesters, No. 84, began his quest in 1964 by asking at least a hundred Jesters if they knew where it had originated. Receiving no answers, he then began to write to the far corners of the earth for information. He finally was told about my account in *Artists of the Tundra and the Sea.* With this in hand, he wrote an account of his search and its results for his fellow members. In his letter to me accompanying the manuscript, he told me about the history and purpose of the Jesters. The Royal Order of Jesters was organized in Honolulu in August 1910 at a Shriners Convention, where one of the participants was wearing an Alaskan ivory billiken that his sister had given him. Then and there, the Shriners adopted it as their symbol. He wrote that (as of 1968) "there are approximately 65 Shrine Temples in the United States, including one in Hawaii, one in Canada and one in Mexico. Our big philanthropy is our 17 Crippled Children Hospitals, and now, three Burns Institutes. Each Shrine Temple has a Jester Court, and the membership is strictly invitational, an applicant must contribute years work [*sic*] in the Shrine. There are over 1,500,000 Shriners and less than 20,000 Jesters" (Carnie A. Generaux to author, Rancho Santa Fe, California, 20 May 1968). He also wrote that "thanks to your writings, now the Billiken has been copyrighted by the Jesters."

References Used

Ahgupuk, George
   1953   *18 Reproductions of Paintings by Alaska's Most Distinguished Artist George Ahgupuk*. Seattle: Deers Press.

Alaska Native Arts Cooperative (ANAC)
   1973   *Catalogue of the Alaska Native Arts and Crafts Cooperative Association, Inc*. Juneau and Anchorage.

Allan, A. A. ("Scotty")
   1931   *Gold, Men and Dogs*. New York and London: G. P. Putnam's Sons.

Almquist, L. Arden
   1962   *Covenant Missions in Alaska*. Chicago: Covenant Press.

ANAC. See Alaska Native Arts Cooperative.

Anderson, H. Dewey, and Walter Crosby Eells
   1935   *Alaska Natives: A Survey of their Sociological and Educational Status*. Stanford: Stanford University Press.

Ard, Saradell. See Frederick, Saradell Ard

Barsness, Kristin J. See Kaplan, Susan, and Kristin J. Barsness

Blaker, Alfred A.
   1980   *Photography: Art and Technique*. San Francisco: W. H. Freeman.

Blaker, Alfred A. See Ray, Dorothy Jean, and Alfred A. Blaker

Bockstoce, John R.
   1986   *Whales, Ice, and Men: The History of Whaling in the Western Arctic*. Seattle: University of Washington Press, in association with the New Bedford Whaling Museum, Massachusetts.

Carpenter, Frank G.
  1916   "Dog Teams Race for Purses of Thousands of Dollars." *Washington (D.C.) Star,* 24 December.

Caswell, Helen
  1968   *Shadows from the Singing House.* Illustrations by Robert Mayokok. Rutland, Vermont: Charles E. Tuttle.

Cole, Terrence
  1984   *Nome, "City of the Golden Beaches."* Jim Walsh, editorial consultant. *Alaska Geographic* 11(1).

Dockstader, Frederick J.
  1960   *Indian Art in America.* Greenwich, Conn.: New York Graphic Society.

Duncan, Kate C.
  1989   *Northern Athapaskan Art: a Beadwork Tradition.* Seattle: University of Washington Press.

Eells, Walter Crosby. See Anderson, H. Dewey, and Walter Crosby Eells.

The Esquimaux
  1867   Issue of June 2, vol. 1, no. 9, published at Libbysville, Port Clarence, Russian America.

Fitzhugh, William W., and Susan A. Kaplan, editors
  1982   *Inua: Spirit World of the Bering Sea Eskimo.* Washington, D.C.: Smithsonian Institution Press.

Frederick, Saradell Ard
  1982   "Roots in the Past:" In *Inua: Spirit World of the Bering Sea Eskimo.* Fitzhugh and Kaplan, editors. Washington, D.C.: Smithsonian Institution Press.

Garber, Clark M.
  1932   "District Superintendent's Report on Eskimos of Yukon-Kuskokwim Delta Coastal Section." Manuscript. Record Group 75, Alaska Division Correspondence 1908–35, National Archives, Washington, D.C.

Geist, Otto William, and Froelich G. Rainey
  1936   *Archaeological Excavations at Kukulik: St. Lawrence Island, Alaska.* Vol. 2, *Miscellaneous Publications of the University of Alaska.* Washington, D.C.: U.S. Government Printing Office.

Green, Paul, with Abbe Abbott
  1959   *I am Eskimo—Aknik my Name.* Illustrations by George Aden Ahgupuk. Juneau: Alaska Northwest Publishing.

Hall, Edwin S., Jr.
  1975   *The Eskimo Storyteller: Folktales from Noatak, Alaska.* Knoxville: University of Tennessee Press.

Hammerich, L.L.
  1977   *A Picture Writing by Edna Kenick, Nunivak, Alaska.* Prefaces by

Jes Asmussen and Robert Petersen. Det Kongelige Danske
Videnskabernes Selskab; Historisk-filosofiske Skrifter 9:1.
Copenhagen; Munksgaard.

Hawkes, Ernest William
1913 *The "Inviting-In" Feast of the Alaskan Eskimo.* Memoir 45, no. 3,
Anthropological Series, Canada Department of Mines, Ottawa.

Heinrich, Albert C.
1950 "Some Present-Day Acculturative Innovations in a Non-literate
Society." *American Anthropologist* 52(2): 235–42.

Henkelman, James W., and Kurt H. Vitt
1985 *Harmonious to Dwell: The History of the Alaska Moravian Church,
1885–1985.* Bethel, Alaska: Moravian Seminary and Archives.

Himmelheber, Hans
1953 *Eskimokünstler.* 2d edition. Eisenach: Erich Röth-Verlag.

1993 *Eskimo Artists.* Translated by Museum Rietberg, Zürich. 1987.
Reprint, Fairbanks: University of Alaska Press.

Hoffman, Walter James
1897 "The Graphic Art of the Eskimos." United States National Museum
Annual Report for 1895. Washington, D.C.: U.S. Government
Printing Office. Pp. 739–968.

Houston, James A.
1951 *Eskimo Handicrafts.* Ottawa: Canadian Handicrafts Guild.

1954 *Canadian Eskimo Art.* Ottawa: Department of Northern Affairs and
National Resources.

Hrdlička, Aleš
1944 *Alaska Diary, 1926–1931.* Lancaster, Pennsylvania: The Jaques
Cattell Press.

Hulbert, Bette
1987 "Note on the Mission of the Sheldon Jackson Museum." In *Faces,
Voices & Dreams: A Celebration of the Centennial of the Sheldon Jackson
Museum.* Peter L. Corey, editor. Juneau. Alaska: Division of Alaska
State Museums.

Indian and Northern Affairs Canada
1992 *Canadian Inuit Sculpture.* Ottawa.

Indian Arts and Crafts Board
1953 *Smoke Signals.* Informational pamphlet. U.S. Department of the
Interior, Washington, D.C.

Israel, Heinz
1961 "Bemerkungen zu Einigen Verzierten Walrosszähnen aus Südwest-
Alaska." Beiträge zur Völkerforschung, Akademie-Verlag, Berlin.

1971 "Beinschnitzerei der Eskimo." Abhandlungen und Berichte des
Staatlichen Museums für Völkerkunde Dresden, Band 33, Berlin.

Kakaruk, John A., and William Oquilluk
    1964   "The Eagle Wolf Dance." Mimeographed pamphlet.

Kaplan, Susan, and Kristin J. Barsness
    1986   *Raven's Journey: The World of Alaska's Native People*. Philadelphia: The
             University Museum, University of Pennsylvania.

Kaplan, Susan, editor. *See* Fitzhugh, William W., and Susan A. Kaplan.

Keithahn, Edward L.
    1945   *Igloo Tales*. Illustrations by George Aden Ahgupuk. Lawrence,
             Kansas: Haskell Institute.

Der Königlichen Museen zu Berlin
    1884   *Amerika's Nordwest-Küste neueste Ergebnisse Ethnologischer Reisen*.
             Catalog of artifacts collected by J. A. Jacobsen in Alaska, 1881–1883.
             Berlin: A. Asher.

Koranda, Lorraine Donoghue
    1972   *Alaskan Eskimo Songs and Stories*. Illustrations by Robert Mayokok.
             For Alaska Festival of Music in cooperation with BP Alaska, Inc.
             Seattle: University of Washington Press. Book and records.

Lantis, Margaret
    1946   *The Social Culture of the Nunivak Eskimo*. Transactions of the
             American Philosophical Society, N.S., vol. 35, part 3, Philadelphia.

    1950   "Mme. Eskimo Proves Herself an Artist." *Natural History* 59(2):68–71.

Lomen, Carl J.
    1954   *Fifty Years in Alaska*. New York: David McKay.

Lucier, Charles
    1994   "Ceremony with Carved Figures for Better Hunting Success."
             Manuscript Consolidation of 1951 field notes.

McDonald, Lucile
    1954   "Pursuer of Alaskan Ivory Carvings," *The Seattle Times*,
             14 November.

McKennan, Robert A.
    1981   "Tanana." In *Handbook of North American Indians,* vol. 6, Subarctic.
             Washington, D.C.: Smithsonian Institution. Pp. 562–76.

Martijn, Charles A.
    1967   "A Retrospective Glance at Canadian Eskimo Carving." *The Beaver,*
             Autumn, Outfit 298: 5–19. Special issue on Eskimo art.

Mason, Otis T.
    1904   *Aboriginal American Basketry: Studies in a Textile Art without Machinery*.
             From U.S. National Museum Report for 1902: 171–548. Reprint,
             Smithsonian Institution Publication no. 128, Washington, D.C.

Mayokok, Robert
    1951a   *Eskimo Customs*. Nome: The Nome Nugget.

1951b   *Eskimo Life: Told by an Eskimo Artist.* Nome: The Nome Nugget.

1959   *True Eskimo Stories.* Sitka: Sitka Printing.

1960   *Eskimo Stories.* Nome: The Nome Nugget.

n.d.   *The Alaskan Eskimo.* Pamphlet. 11 pages.

Morgan, Lael

1988   *Art and Eskimo Power: The Life and Times of Alaskan Howard Rock.* Fairbanks: Epicenter Press.

National Gallery of Art

1973   *The Far North: 2000 Years of American Eskimo and Indian Art.* Catalog Washington, D.C.

Nelson, Edward William

1899   *The Eskimo About Bering Strait.* Bureau of American Ethnology report, vol. 18, part 1, Washington, D.C.

Oquilluk, William. *See* Kakaruk, John A., and William Oquilluk.

Patty, Stanton H.

1971   "A Conference with the Tanana Chiefs." *Alaska Journal* 1(2):2–18.

Rainey, Froelich

1959   "The Vanishing Art of the Arctic." *Expedition* 1(2):3–13.

Rainey, Froelich G. See Geist, Otto William, and Froelich G. Rainey.

Ray, Dorothy Jean

1960   "The Mystery of the Billiken." *Alaska Sportsman* 26(9):36–37, 56.

1961   *Artists of the Tundra and the Sea.* Seattle: University of Washington Press. Reprint edition, 1980.

1964   "Nineteenth Century Settlement and Subsistence Patterns in Bering Strait. *Arctic Anthropology* 2(2):61–94.

1967a   "Land Tenure and Polity of the Bering Strait Eskimos." *Journal of the West* 6(3):371–94.

1967b   "Rock Paintings on the Tuksuk." *Alaska Sportsman* 33(8):31–34.

1968   "Taking the Census in 1900." *Alaska Sportsman* 34(10):10–13, 42–43.

1969   *Graphic Arts of the Alaskan Eskimo.* Native American Arts 2, U. S. Department of the Interior. Washington, D.C.: Indian Arts and Crafts Board.

1971a   "The Bible in Picture Writing." *The Beaver,* Autumn, Outfit 302, no. 2, pp. 20–24.

1971b   "Eskimo Place-names in Bering Strait and Vicinity." *Names* 19(1):1-33.

1971c   "Kakarook, Eskimo Artist." *Alaska Journal* 1(1):8–15, cover. Nine Kakarook paintings reproduced in color.

1974   "The Billiken." *Alaska Journal* 4(1):25–31.

1975   *The Eskimos of Bering Strait, 1650–1898.* Seattle: University of Washington Press. Paperback edition, 1992.

1976   "The Kheuveren Legend." *Alaska Journal* 6(3):146–53.

1977   *Eskimo Art: Tradition and Innovation in North Alaska.* Seattle: University of Washington Press.

1981   *Aleut and Eskimo Art: Tradition and Innovation in South Alaska.* Seattle: University of Washington Press.

1982a   "Mortuary Art of the Alaskan Eskimos." *American Indian Art Magazine* 7(2):50–57.

1982b   "Reflections in Ivory." In *Inua: Spirit World of the Bering Sea Eskimo.* Fitzhugh and Kaplan, editors. Washington, D.C.: Smithsonian Institution Press. Pp. 254–67.

1983   *Ethnohistory in the Arctic: The Bering Strait Eskimo.* Kingston, Ontario: The Limestone Press.

1984a   "Happy Jack: King of the Eskimo Ivory Carvers." *American Indian Art Magazine* 10(1):32–47, 77.

1984b   "Sinrock Mary: From Eskimo Wife to Reindeer Queen." *Pacific Northwest Quarterly* 75(3):98–107.

1984c   "The Sinuk Mission: Experiment in Eskimo Relocation and Acculturation." *Alaska History* 1(1):27–43.

1984d   "Bering Strait Eskimo." In *Handbook of North American Indians,* vol. 5, Arctic. Washington, D.C.: Smithsonian Institution. Pp. 285–302.

1989   "Happy Jack and his Artistry." *American Indian Art Magazine* 15(1):40–53.

1992   "Beyond Souvenirs: a Forty-five-year Odyssey through Eskimo Art." In *Bering and Chirikov: The American Voyages and their Impact.* O. W. Frost, editor. Anchorage: Alaska Historical Society. Pp. 366–78.

Ray, Dorothy Jean, editor
1966   "The Eskimo of St. Michael and Vicinity as Related by H. M. W. Edmonds." Introduction and notes by D. J. Ray. *Anthropological Papers of the University of Alaska* 13(1).

Ray, Dorothy Jean, and Alfred A. Blaker
1967   *Eskimo Masks: Art and Ceremony.* Photographs by Alfred A. Blaker. Seattle: University of Washington Press. Paperback edition, 1975. Danish translation, 1970.

Renner, Louis L., S. J.
1979   *Pioneer Missionary to the Bering Strait Eskimos: Bellarmine Lafortune, S. J.* With Dorothy Jean Ray, for the Alaska Historical Commission. Portland, Oregon: Binford and Mort.

Schmitt, Alfred
    1951   *Die Alaska-Schrift und ihre Schriftgeschichtliche Bedeutung.* Marburg: Simons Verlag.

Smith, James G. E.
    1980   *Arctic Art: Eskimo Ivory.* New York: Museum of the American Indian, Heye Foundation. Exhibition catalog.

Smoke Signals.
    See Indian Arts and Crafts Board

Sotheby's
    1983   *Fine American Indian Art.* Catalog, Sale 5096, 22 October, New York.

    1988   *Important American Indian Art.* Catalog, Sale 5785, November 29, New York.

    1991   *Fine American Indian Art.* Catalog, Sale 6245, November 26, New York.

    1993   *Fine American Indian Art.* Catalog, Sale 6510, December 4, New York.

Stefansson, Evelyn
    1943   *Here is Alaska.* New York: Charles Scribner's Sons.

Swinton, George
    1972   *Sculpture of the Eskimo.* Toronto: McClelland and Stewart.

Thornton, Harrison R.
    1931   *Among the Eskimos of Wales, Alaska.* Baltimore: Johns Hopkins Press.

University of Alaska
    1964   *Alaska Native Arts and Crafts Potential for Expansion: Final Report to Bureau of Indian Affairs* [Fairbanks].

VanStone, James W.
    1974   *Athapaskan Adaptations.* Chicago: Aldine

    1976   *The Bruce Collection of Eskimo Material Culture from Port Clarence, Alaska.* Fieldiana: Anthropology 67. Chicago: Field Museum of Natural History.

    1980   *The Bruce Collection of Eskimo Material Culture from Kotzebue Sound, Alaska.* Fieldiana. Anthropology. New series, no. 1. Chicago: Field Museum of Natural History.

Varjola, Pirjo
    1990   *The Etholén Collection.* With contributions by Julia P. Averkieva and Roza G. Liapunova. Helsinki: National Board of Antiquities.

Vitt, Kurt H. See Henkelman, James W., and Kurt H. Vitt

Zagoskin, L. A.
    1967   *Lieutenant Zagoskin's Travels in Russian America, 1842–1844.* Edited by Henry N. Michael. Translated by Penelope Rainey. Arctic Institute of North America, Anthropology of the North: Translations from Russian Sources, no. 7. Toronto: University of Toronto Press.

Acknowledgments

In my books, papers, and articles I have thanked people who have given me information or helped in other ways during my research and writing, and in this book—which is somewhat of a culmination of all that work—I was tempted to list everyone again, but the eyes begin to wander after reading the first dozen, so I am acknowledging here only those directly involved in the preparation of this book. Others who have contributed to the collection in many ways are, of course, mentioned in the text.

I am grateful to the following people for their help: Mardonna Austin-McKillop; Lois Rayne Bark; John R. Bockstoce; Ann Chandonnet; Terrence Cole; Peter L. Corey; Dennis Corrington; Stuart M. Frank; David A. Hales; Marge Heath; Dorothy and Maurice Kamen-Kaye; Eleanor Klingel; Margaret Lantis; Dinah W. Larsen; Frieda Larsen; Iris Foster Magnell; Bruce Merrell; Caroline McLain Reader; Louis L. Renner, S.J.; Judy Robertson; Jane Schuldberg; Kathleen Lopp Smith; and Walter A. Van Horn. Wanda W. Chin, Terry Dickey, Aldona Jonaitis, and Barry McWayne are directly involved in the exhibition.

I also want to thank Verne F. Ray for reading the manuscript before I submitted it to the University of Washington Press, which has published the majority of my books. The editors there, beginning in 1961 with the publication of *Artists of the Tundra and the Sea,* have always maintained the integrity of my manuscripts and have avoided what H. G. Wells has termed a passion unequaled by any in the world: "the passion to alter someone else's manuscript." So, thanks to the hands-on editors these past thirty years: Naomi Pascal, Marilyn Trueblood, Gretchen Van Meter, and Marilyn Waesche.

Index

Note: The index contains subject matter in figures, illustrations, and some captions.

boards

Tutut: etching (by Bernard Katexac), described and illustrated, 35–37

Twined basketry, 58